THE FIELD
BOOK of COUNTRY QUERIES

THE FIELD

BOOK of COUNTRY QUERIES

Quiller

Copyright © 2011 IPC Media Ltd
Illustrations © 2011 Kerry Lemon

First published in the UK in 2011
by Quiller, an imprint of Quiller Publishing Ltd

British Library Cataloguing-in-Publication Data
A catalogue record for this book
is available from the British Library

ISBN 978 1 84689 099 4

Illustrations by Kerry Lemon
Designed and typeset by Paul Saunders

Printed in Malta by Gutenberg Press Ltd

Quiller

An imprint of Quiller Publishing Ltd
Wykey House, Wykey, Shrewsbury, SY4 1JA
Tel: 01939 261616 Fax: 01939 261606
E-mail: info@quillerbooks.com
Website: www.countrybooksdirect.com

Contents

Note

FROM THE ARCHIVES

The items appearing under this heading appeared in early editions of *The Field*. They are reproduced for interest only and any advice should not necessarily be heeded today.

Foreword

There was a moment when *The Field* and Radio 1 collided briefly. A reader had asked our Country Queries editor for a foolproof method of disposing of the moles transforming his lawn into a workmanlike model of the Himalayan foothills. Our lady recommended the usual array of formidable traps but her suggestion was trumped by another reader, who'd discovered that moles would flee instantly if piped a constant stream of Radio 1, volume turned to high.

Radio 1, suitably flattered by a mention in *The Field*, then set about compiling the Mole Catcher's Top Ten. Naturally, this included most tracks from the Velvet Underground and Elvis Presley's The Green Green Grass to Roam but the winner, by a substantial margin, was The Clash's I Fought The Lawn (And the Lawn Won).

Field readers always have the solution to a problem, whether it's a pattern for kilt socks (Patons No 3285) or cleaning out a vacuum flask (bicarb of soda), and they have always been more than forthcoming with robust advice; you should not, perhaps, ask a *Field* reader for the best way to cure a sick guinea pig.

The majority of the answers however, have been hunted down by our Country Queries editors, those selfless stalwarts who settle down to the daily mound of letters with the dedication of Bletchley Park code-breakers.

Under my editorship, there have been two such paragons: Christina Grindon and Rosie Macdonald. Together they have manned the Country Queries desk with style and charm, remaining totally unflustered even when some of the queries have bordered on the bizarre. (A ban still exists on the topic of fishing flies and female pheromones.)

Their work fills much of this book, put together with panache by the Quiller Publishing team under the guidance of Alexandra Henton of *The Field*.

Mostly, however, this book is the creation of *Field* readers, whose appetite for knowledge and enthusiasm in sharing it has sustained the magazine for more than 150 years. The result is indispensable to everyone who faces the daily challenges of living in a country house.

Jonathan Young, Editor

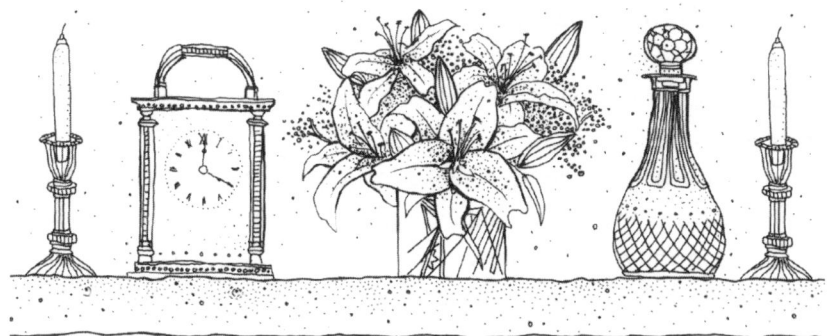

Household

Copper Shine

Q. I have a circular copper dish approximately 30cm (1ft) deep and 45cm (1½ft) wide in which I grow plants. It sits in the garden and is now completely black. I would like to get it cleaned so the original copper colour shows through, and then cover it in some form of varnish to prevent it re-tarnishing. Where might I get this work done?

SS, Farnham, Hants

A. Copper that has turned black from the weather may need to be polished by machine to bring back its original hue. Brass Master specialises in the repair, cleaning and production of items in brass, copper and bronze. The firm would polish this item by hand on a three-phase polishing lathe, which would return its original mirror finish. Firstly, a string mop and special soap would cut through the black grime; followed by the application of a stitch mop and polishing soap that would help its shine return; and ending with a soft mop and rouge polishing soap for the original mirror finish. To help keep this finish the dish could be sprayed with a clear lacquer but the lacquer cannot be guaranteed for items kept outside; it would last very much longer indoors. The process would take an hour and cost approximately £70.

Call Brass Master on 07713526495 or visit www.brassmaster. co.uk.

Another method for less stained copper is: Sprinkle coarse salt on to half a lemon and rub the copper vigorously. Wipe with a damp cloth and polish with a soft dry one.

Reader's top tips

DECANTER

To clean a narrow-necked decanter, fill it with lukewarm water and plunge vigorously with a bunch of stinging nettles (best to wear gloves).

B Ashton, Derbyshire

Stains on Steel

Q. I am contemplating bringing a set of 18th-century silver-handled knives back into use. What can I use to polish the non-stainless knife blades?

MCM, Sudbury, Suffolk

A. Steel knives are very hard to keep clean and shiny as they are affected by water and dampness which cause rust. Before the invention of stainless steel Victorian maids used a special machine, the Kent knife cleaner, to polish them. The knives would be put blade down into holes along the top of the machine with a small amount of polishing powder. A handle was then turned to move hard brushes inside the machine that removed pitting on the blades and polished them up.

It is still possible to purchase the Kent knife cleaner at auction or at a general antique/junk shop. Alternatively, the blades can be cleaned by using a burnt cork and charcoal but if they are very rusty they might require some professional treatment first. As steel knives are susceptible to rust you might consider spraying the blades with WD-40 after use. This can be wiped off before re-use.

Wasp Wash

Q. Wasps have been stripping the surface of our outdoor teak furniture over the past couple of years. Do you know of something that would deter them without killing any other insects that might land on it?

TJ, Sibbertoft, Leicestershire

A. Wasps build their nests from pulp gathered from the scraping and eating of wood. They attack garden furniture and leave marks which will scrub and weather out. These can be removed with a scrubbing brush and water. This is easier if the furniture has been thoroughly wetted and allowed to stand for 20 minutes to soften any surface dirt. After scrubbing allow the teak to dry fully before sanding very lightly with glass paper. Then wash the furniture with a very strong solution of Dettol and water. If the wasps have been regularly attacking the wood you may have a nest nearby.

Reader's top tips

WASPS

To stop alfresco dining from being spoiled by wasps cover an old jam-jar, still containing something sweet, tightly with cling film and make a small hole in the top. The stinging nasties will crawl in for a feast and be trapped.

Mrs V Cross, Cumbria

Cap Repair

Q. I have a much loved tweed cap bought from Lock & Co of St James's about 15 years ago, which is in need of repair and attention. It also has a thin rim of dirt and grease at the bottom outside edge of the cap. Lock's tell me that the person who used to do its repairs has retired and does not know anybody else who can do them. Can you help?

DR, Alton, Hampshire

A. Lock's is happy to undertake repair work on tweed caps that have been purchased relatively recently but does not undertake work on caps of this vintage. This is party due to the fact that the fabric might have perished, any tweed used would be of a different colour and quality due to its age and the general overall finished effect might not fit the high standards for which Lock's is known. It offers the following advice for home care: clean off all mud and dirt when dry by using a pure bristle hat brush and steam from a kettle if necessary; stubborn grease marks can be removed by using a spirit such as lighter fuel or dry cleaning fluid, but test a small area inside the cap first; and maintain the cap size by inserting a hat jack (available from Lock's) inside, adjusting to a close fit and leaving in a wet or steamed cap until dry.

It is worth approaching your local dry-cleaners to see whether it offers an efficient mending service – many do. Alternatively, go to www.lockhatters.co.uk or visit its stand at the Game Fair to invest in a new cap.

Reader's top tips

POLLEN STAINS

If disaster strikes and you get staining lily pollen on your clothes, carefully use Sellotape to lift off the grains and save your shirt or jumper. Keep lifting with fresh tape until the pollen has gone.

W Bedford, Kent

Putty Put-Off

Q. Recently I had the windows renewed on one side of my house at great expense as magpies had eaten the putty out of the windows. The work was finished one week and the next week they had eaten all the putty again. What can I do to make the putty less appealing for the wretched birds?

SR, Royston, Cambridgeshire

A. This is a relatively common problem as the magpies are attracted to the linseed oil, an ingredient in the putty. The RSPB suggests a variety of solutions. You could use an alternative putty such as Arbolite, or paint the putty with a bird repellent that contains aluminium ammonium sulphate (available from hardware stores, pet shops and garden centres). This makes the putty unpalatable but does not harm the birds. Since the problem is sometimes caused by the magpie seeing its reflection in the window and pecking at the putty and glass to try and get through to its opponent, covering the glass and putty with cling film can help prevent this. You can also hang old CDs and strips of foil on fishing wire across the window when waiting for the putty to harden, which should be enough to deter the magpies. Birds often develop habits and this spell of intervention should be enough to break their obsession with it.

Professional painters and glaziers solve the problem of birds attacking new putty for its linseed oil content by painting the putty over with a white lead paint as soon as the surface has hardened slightly. It seems to work most of the time but not infallibly, depending how hungry and determine the birds are.

Alternatively, use one of the synthetic types of putty or sealants which are a little more expensive but more durable than linseed oil putty. Another solution might be to add pepper to the putty to deter the magpies, or cover it with sealant tape or sheets of polythene.

Take the Heat Off

Q. I would like to remove heat stains from my mahogany table which was damaged by having hot plates put on it. Is there a product available on the market to remove these?

SM, Odenthal, Germany

A. There are two products available to buy that help remove heat marks. Liberon Ring Remover will remove most white watermarks and heat marks from polished surfaces including French polishes, varnishes and lacquers. It is non-colouring. Visit www.liberon.co.uk for details of stockists.

Antiquax Ring Remover is a blend of oil and turpentines that removes most heat marks from polished furniture, the website is www.antiquax. info. Both of these products should be tried first on a small, discreet area to ensure they are suitable for your piece of furniture. If the marks made by water or heat are dark they indicate damage to the wood, in which case contact a furniture restorer before you proceed.

..... Reader's top tips ....

METHS

To remove watermarks, moisten a pad of cotton wool with methylated spirits, add a drop of linseed oil as a lubricant. Wrap paid in a double thickness of butter muslin and gently rub the stain.

S Martin, Horsham, Sussex

Extending Flower Life

Q. Is there an ingenious way of extending the life of cut flowers? I am usually given a few bunches by visitors over Christmas and feel embarrassed at sometimes having to bin them before the guest departs.

CT, by e-mail

A. There are various items you can add to the water of cut flowers or flower arrangements to extend their life. A crushed aspirin placed in the water before the flowers are added to the vase; a teaspoon of sugar, a pinch of salt and teaspoon of baking powder; a multivitamin tablet; and a copper coin may help the flowers last longer. It is still important to make sure the vase has been well cleaned first and that the water is changed regularly.

Reader's top tips

CANDLES

To increase the burning time of candles, put them in the freezer for a while before they are used.

Neville Smith, Monmouth, Gwent

Bad Hair Days

Q. A local cat has been breaking into our house by squeezing through any window we leave open, no matter how small the gap. Though we have virtually cured this problem, we can't seem to get rid of the excess cat hair left behind. It appears to be stuck to various chairs and a vacuum doesn't remove it despite the manufacturer's claims. Can you help?

CKB, Steeple Bumpstead, Suffolk

A. A quick and efficient way to remove cat hair from upholstery is by using a rubber glove that has a raised grip on its palm. Put the glove on, dampen it, then rub in short scraping motions against the fabric. The cat hair will stick to the glove. This also works using a damped sponge. If you are concerned about the upholstery getting slightly damp, test a small area first to see whether it marks.

Moths Galore

Q. I have lost five suits and numerous woollen garments to a plague of moths. Mothballs and other products have failed. Have you any killer ideas?

DP, London

A. To prevent and reduce moth infestation, regularly vacuum under beds, in wardrobes, along skirting boards and under furniture that is not moved often. Moths dislike light and disturbance. Their life cycle is about 21 days, so every month open drawers, vacuum corners, shake out clothing and, on a sunny day, hang suits outside to air. Never put clothes away dirty as this will make an attack more likely. When storing clothes make sure they have been cleaned and put them away in sealed plastic bags. To work in parallel with the cleaning use a moth repellent such as lavender oil liberally soaked into handkerchiefs and hung in the wardrobe at intervals or smeared on paper and put in drawers. Santa Maria Novella, London

SW3, tel 020 7460 6600, sells an oil, Cartine Odorose preservare la Lana, infused with lavender, cedar and mint, which you apply to acid-free cards and hang from the hangers. Both methods keep cupboards and drawers fresh and moth-free. For a serious infestation Rentokil has a powerful range of insecticides and can treat areas for you to ensure the problem has been dealt with fully. Then start afresh using lavender oil as a preventive measure. Call Rentokil on 0800 218 2210.

See also Reader's Top Tips below

Reader's top tips

MOTHS

To keep moths from destroying your favourite cashmere jumpers collect some conkers and pack them among clothes in drawers or string them from wardrobe rails. Conkers are also effective in repelling spiders. They needn't be obvious; hide them behind furniture or in corners and watch your spider population wither away. They may return when the conkers dry up. In simpler times conkers were carried in coat pockets to help prevent piles and rheumatism.

Sheila Faulks, York

Reader's top tips

MOTH DAMAGE

To prevent moth damage freeze cashmere jumpers for a week and then store with lavender.

Mrs Watts, Leicestershire

Freshening Flasks

Q. I have an assortment of flasks, mainly stainless steel, which have had a lot of use over the summer and they all seem to have retained certain odours. I would like to know exactly how I should clean them to ensure that they stay fresh. Can I put them in the dishwasher?

TG, by e-mail

A. Firstly clean the stainless steel or glass-lined flask with washing-up liquid and warm water to remove the residual contents. For basic staining and odour removal fill the flask with a large teaspoon of bicarbonate of soda and hot water, secure the lid tightly and leave overnight, then rinse well. If the problem is excessive repeat the same process with a normal household scale remover or a denture tablet. Always soak overnight and rinse well before use. If the flasks are used on a weekly basis, full cleaning is ideally performed once a week to prevent a build-up of stains and odour. The moist, dark environment of a flask is an ideal place for mould spores to grow, so flasks should always be stored with their lids off. Thermos UK says flasks must not be put in the dishwasher, immersed in water or have any abrasive or bleach products used in them.

.... *Reader's top tips* ....

TEA AND COFFEE STAINS

To remove tea and coffee stains from a stainless steel flask put one dishwasher tablet in the flask with hot water overnight. Then rinse out.

P M Drummond, Whitebridge, Inverness-shire

Soap Saver

Q. As operators of a farmhouse bed and breakfast we are constantly inundated with small pieces of slightly used, good-quality soap. Is there a good way of recycling them into larger blocks for our own use?

PDM, Newnham Bridge, Worcs

A. There are various uses for those remaining bits of soap. To recycle the small pieces to make a large bar, place them in a saucepan, cover with water and allow to soak for 24 hours. Bring to the boil, stirring occasionally. Remove from the heat and add a tablespoon of vegetable oil to each cupful of soap mixture. Pour this into suitable moulds and allow to harden for 10 to 14 days before use. If you want to use the soap after 24 hours then leave out the vegetable oil.

Leftover pieces can also be used to make liquid soap. Place the scraps of soap in a jar of hot water, add a dash of lemon juice and glycerine and shake well. Leftover soap can be used to make an all-purpose stain remover too. Chop four cupfuls of the soap and place them in a saucepan with three tablespoons of eucalyptus oil, a cup of methylated spirits and a cup of boiling water. Stand the saucepan in a larger pan of hot water over a medium heat, stirring the mixture until it turns clear. Pour the soap into moulds and allow to cool. The soap takes about four weeks to harden fully.

It is important not to mix soaps of different shades as the end colour can be unpleasant.

Reader's top tips

SPLINTERS

To remove splinters or thorns without using a needle, place some soft soap in the pad of a plaster, sprinkle brown sugar on to the soap and apply the plaster over the area. After a day or so the splinter should come out.

Sarah Gammage, Guilsborough, Northamptonshire

Mistletoe Ball

Q. We are lucky to have good crops of accessible mistletoe growing in trees near us. Every year I decorate the house with bunches but this year I would like to try something different, perhaps trying to shape it into a ball. Have you any suggestions on how to do this in a simple way and so it doesn't fall apart?

RJH, by e-mail

A. I have taken advice from a florist who suggests using a pre-soaked oasis ball that has been left to drain. Make a hole through the centre of the foam ball with a knitting needle or skewer and push a length of decorative ribbon through and out the other side. Tie the end of the ribbon to a small piece of wood, which will act as a toggle. Cover the foam ball with moss, securing it with florist wire bent like a hair-pin. Spear the moss ball with pieces of mistletoe and continue until the ball is well covered. Using the foam also ensures that the mistletoe lasts for longer. You can add crystal droplets and extra ribbons should you wish.

Maximising Mask Life

Q. I have been given a fox mask. The mask was well preserved and mounted in 1936 having been caught by the Cattistock pack. It rather lacks lustre and in particular the teeth are very yellow. How can I improve it?

DL, Skipton, N.Yorks

A. If the mount or mask is damaged in any way the most efficient method of ensuring its continued longevity is to approach a local taxidermist who will patch, fill and groom as necessary. Otherwise check for signs of insect infestation and if you find any, cure it by freezing the mask for two weeks at a temperature of minus 20°C or using chemicals relating to the insect, which can be bought at hardware stores.

To protect against moths make a small incision in a discreet part of the mask and push in a moth ball. To clean the fur set the nozzle on your Hoover to blow rather than suck as this will gently remove all dust and dirt. Then brush the fur gently with a soft brush. If the fur still appears dull lightly sponge with either a dry-cleaning fluid or a mild detergent. Don't soak or immerse the mask in water.

The teeth can be cleaned by gently rubbing them with either wire wool or a small wire brush and methylated spirits. You might need to repeat the process a few times to achieve a reasonable colour. This should rejuvenate the mask sufficiently to provide you with years of pleasure.

Reader's top tips

UNSHRINK WOOLLIES

To unshrink a sweater, soak for 15 minutes in a sink of luke-warm water with 2tbsp of baby shampoo. Roll in a towel to absorb moisture, pin to a cork board and stretch to size. Repeat every few hours until dry.

Lucy Frampton, by e-mail

Reader's top tips

GUMBOOTS

If gumboots are wet and smelly, a quick solution is to cut a boot shape in a good-quality carrier bag, tape the open seam, apart from the top and toe and put it in the boot. Taking care not to get it all too hot, blow a hair-drier down the boot for a few minutes. Don't let it melt the bag. If you have more time, warm newspaper is a very good start to the process.

John Clements, by e-mail

Tennis Courts Gather Moss

Q. Apart from Jeyes Fluid or a biological soap powder has anyone got any good ideas on how to remove moss from the surface of hard tennis courts?

MLS, Woodbridge, Suffolk

A. Hard tennis courts that suffer from moss should ideally be cleaned twice a year when the temperature is above 10°C. The position of the court and amount of shade play an enormous part in the build-up of moss and its requirement for regular cleaning. Jeyes Fluid or biological powder can damage the surface of the court and it is advisable to spray the court with a fungicide instead. Most garden centres or nurseries supply suitable sprays for moss and one would need three litres (5 pints) of fungicide to 60 litres (13 gallons) of water approximately to spray one court. These sprays are weaker than commercial sprays, but are still efficient.

You can pressure wash the surface of the court and then spray it with a suitable product, ensuring the weather will be fine for a minimum of two hours but ideally dry for 24 hours before you do so. The whole process should take a couple of days, with the court being ready to use immediately and the moss dying within 14 to 21 days.

Candle Wax

Q. Can you please come to my help and salvage my marriage? Over Christmas I spilt candle wax across a natural stone hearth fireplace and have found it difficult to remove completely. I can't convince my wife that the candle wax enhances the character of a family home.

DVW, Codsall, Staffordshire

A. Marriage can be a tricky business without the extra problem of candle wax, but all is not lost. I suggest using an extremely sharp knife to scrape off the surface wax before lightly sanding the area with fine sandpaper.

Storing Holly

Q. It seems that every year the birds strip our holly trees of berries at just the wrong time. Is there a good way to store holly if you cut it early for Christmas? Also when is a good time to shape and prune unruly bushes?

CS, by e-mail

A. Suppliers of holly cut it as soon as the berries are ripe and place it in cold storage with adjustable light and temperature, but this method is virtually impossible for most of us to copy. Instead, start by keeping an eye on the birds' activity and cutting the holly as late as possible.

Insert the cut branches close together in the ground so that they can take up as much moisture as they require from the soil. Cover them with a fine mesh netting and bury the edges in the ground to ensure mice or birds cannot get in. For extra protection, place a few mouse traps among the holly.

Another method of storing is to place the cut branches in buckets of water in a cool shed. However, keep the branches away from any stored vegetables or fruit as the latter release a gas called ethylene, which will 'ripen' the holly. Depending on the size of your holly bush, you can also net or partially net the tree directly. The birds might damage the outside berries slightly but the majority will remain intact.

Because the flower buds are formed in late summer, any pruning and shaping should be undertaken in spring or early summer to avoid cutting away next year's flowers and, consequently, berries. It is always a good idea to keep the base of the holly tree open to air and light as it ensures that there is no dying back of the lower branches. These vulnerable branches can suffer from a fungus that attacks feeble twigs in the damp and shade.

Bonkers about Conkers

Q. Autumn brings the conker season and with it great demands on my memory of how to harden the conkers. My great-grandson is desperate for a champion conker and it has been a few decades since I have had the delight of playing. Can you help?

JS-B, Droitwich, Worcestershire

A. Collecting conkers for the forthcoming season has to be one of the major highlights of the autumn for the young (and old). The best conkers are those that are just ripe but haven't fallen. They should be slightly smaller than a golf ball.

There are numerous ways of conker hardening, though some border on cheating. The traditional method is to drill holes in the conker and leave in the airing cupboard for a year, by which time it will be rock hard.

If this is your first conker season you will need a quicker method. Soak the conker in vinegar for a good hour and then bake in the hot oven for five to 10 minutes. Don't leave them to roast and go black; all you are trying to do is speed up the drying process. Alternatively, place in a cool oven overnight. Remember to make the holes in the conkers before you embark on the hardening process and don't forget to collect extra conkers to store for next year.

.... *Reader's top tips* ....

BLOCKED GULLIES

An empty fertiliser bag or large plastic bag is brilliant for unblocking rainwater gullies with a U-bend. Fill the drain with water, stuff the bag down the gully, then pull it out as quickly as possible. Repeat several times as necessary. It has the same effect as a plunger.

William May Somerville, Devon

Spout Cleaning

Q. We have a silver teapot which we use daily. Large pieces of tannin have started coming out of the spout. How can I remove the encrusted tannin from that area?

RDW, by e-mail

A. The Silver Trust was set up in 1987 as a registered charity. It encourages and publicises the work of practising British silversmiths, with many of the silversmiths receiving commissions as a result.

Christopher English of the Trust kindly offers the following advice: use one from a choice of three substances to remove the tannin; two tablespoons of bicarbonate of soda, a Steradent tablet or a vinegar/water solution mixed in equal measures. In each case put your chosen cleaner in the bowl of the teapot, fill with warm water and leave overnight. The following morning use a spout brush to clean the spout gently and rinse well. Mr English warns that if the spout is severely clogged with tannin you might find the silver underneath is badly pitted and could easily end up with leaks, so take it carefully. Most hardware shops sell spout brushes.

Reader's top tips

TEAPOT

To keep a unused teapot fresh put a dry tea bag in it.

Jean Grieve, Farnborough

Beeswax Polish

Q. I have been given 2kg of beeswax. Can you suggest a simple recipe for furniture polish?

LW-S, Selby, North Yorkshire

A. David Bates of Camelot Country Products tells me that turpentine and beeswax make a good polish; the addition of carnauba wax is not necessary. Use real turpentine and not substitutes.

To make: put equal amounts of beeswax (broken into small pieces) and turpentine (for example, 100g (4oz) and 100ml (3½ fl oz) respectively) into a large jam jar and put the lid on. Place somewhere warm until the wax has dissolved into the turpentine, which takes a few days. Then transfer into smaller jars or tins ensuring the lids provide a good seal to prevent the turpentine evaporating. Alternatively, you could melt the wax, add the turpentine and immediately pour into tins or preheated jars to set.

Always melt the wax using a water bath: place a small saucepan of wax inside the larger pan of water. Never place a pan of wax directly on a hot plate or ring. Beeswax will not boil but just get hotter and hotter until it ignites. Turpentine is flammable and the melted wax should be kept well away from the heat source when the turpentine is added. Heed the health warnings that come with turpentine.

To use: for polished wood, apply the wax sparingly with a cloth or soft brush. Leave for about 20 minutes to allow penetration of the wood then polish with a soft cloth. Doing this every few months should be enough. For unpolished wood, apply a few coats of sanding sealer, available from hardware shops, as per the instructions, then a reasonable amount of beeswax polish and give it a good, hard polish every day for about a week. Then use as for polished wood.

David Bates supplies beeswax in blocks or granulated, his own beeswax polish, wild-flower honey and beekeeping books and equipment; he is happy to give beekeeping advice. Contact Camelot Country Products, Curry Rivel, Langport, Somerset TA10 0HB, tel 01458 253098, www.honeyshop.co.uk.

Beeswax Balsam

Q. Do you know of a recipe for what Mother called beeswax balsam for polishing wood? Apart from beeswax, I'm sure the mixture contained turpentine.

RS, Braunton, Devon

A. Fosse Way Honey gave me the following recipe. Put a pint of genuine turpentine into a jar and add 100g (4oz) shredded beeswax and 25g (1oz) shredded white candle wax to it. Cover and leave it somewhere warm to dissolve for 48 hours. Then mix 50g (2oz) grated Lux soap in 150ml (¼ pint) of warm water, and amalgamate with the dissolved waxes. Add two tablespoons of vinegar and mix well. Pour the resulting cream into suitable jars and store. This cream provides a lasting polish that feeds the wood and will withstand the damp. Beeswax in 100g (4oz) blocks is available from Fosse Way Honey. The company also sells beeswax furniture cream. Contact Fosse Way Honey, Northcote, Deppers Bridge, Southam, Warwickshire CV47 2SU tel 01295 780054.

..... *Reader's top tips* ....

CARTON RECYCLING

Tetra Pak and similar coated cartons cannot be recycled with paper and there are few specialist recycling facilities for them. However, they make excellent firelighters. Wash, allow to dry thoroughly, then scrunch up and light the opened end.

David Starbuck-Edwards, Chester

Bath Infusions

Q. We have a good selection of herbs in the garden, more than we can eat or dry. We'd like to use some to make scented baths but are not sure how to go about it. Can you help?

GLR, Emerson's Green, Avon

A. Put a good handful of a freshly picked single herb or a mixture of up to four different herbs in the middle of a piece of muslin or fine gauze and draw up the corners into a bag. Tie securely adding a loop long enough to hang over the hot tap so that the bag sits in the running water. The essential oils will be drawn out by the heat. Chamomile, jasmine and valerian make relaxing baths, basil, rosemary, thyme and lemon verbena are stimulating and calendula and comfrey are healing. There are so many uses for herbs, from disinfectants, fly-away posies and rinse-waters to scented ink, aromatic beads, pomanders and skin cleaners that it is worth investing in a good book, such as *The Complete Book of Herbs* by Lesley Bremness.

Aga Cleaning

Q. How do you get the hard baked-on grease off an Aga? All the experts seem to say don't let it get baked on, mop up all splashes with a wet cloth and so on. But in the real world, fat does spit and does get baked on hard. I reckon you need a mild solution of caustic soda but what is the right strength and should it be made with cold, warm or hot water?

CMY, Plymouth, Devon

A. Aga says that in the oven any grease should burn off and therefore not need cleaning. For the enamel it does, as you say, suggest cleaning before it gets baked on but also suggests its own vitreous enamel cleaner.

Caustic soda is a dangerous substance and should not be used; baking soda is also inappropriate but Dri-Pak, which manufactures soda crystals (in effect, washing soda), says that a solution of soda crystals and water is effective for a myriad of things, including the removal of burnt-on food and grease from pans and cookers (inside and out). The exception is aluminium on which it should not be used.

Dri-Pak confirms it is OK to use a soda solution on the vitreous enamel of an Aga but says that if the Aga is permanently on and therefore permanently hot, a soda solution would dry too quickly and leave white marks. In this case you should use Dri-Pak ready-to-use liquid soda, which comes in a spray bottle and has added ingredients to stop this happening. Apart from a permanently hot Aga, use the spray on a cold oven.

To make a strong soda solution for pans and cookers, use 150g (5 oz) of soda crystals to 500ml (¾ pint) of hot water. For badly burnt-on grease or food leave to soak a little while before wiping off, and repeat the process until clean.

Liquid soda and/or soda solution in varying strengths has a wide range of uses including removing tannin stains from teapots and cups, removing odours and stains from chopping boards, removing grease and lime scale from baths, and keeping waste pipes clear. For a comprehensive leaflet on what soda can be used for, call Dri-Pak on 0115 932 5165 or visit its website, www.dripak.co.uk.

... *Reader's top tips* ....

PUMICE STONE

Gently rub lime scale that has accumulated on chrome bath taps with pumice stone.

Sue Tunnard, King's Lynn, Norfolk

Wasps in the Attic

Q. As we are plagued each year by wasps nesting in the roof of our house, I wonder whether you can recommend a wasp deterrent. Each year the pest-control people deal with the nests but we really need to find a deterrent since a member of the family is seriously allergic to wasp stings.

PS, Kidderminster, Worcs

A. John Peacock of Basingstoke & District Beekeepers' Association tells me that the wasps' cycle begins in the winter with a queen wasp that finds a shed or loft to hibernate in. Early in spring, she will wake and lay just a few eggs; these will hatch and begin to make a nest, then as more eggs are laid and hatched so the nest grows.

There is no deterrent that will keep the queen from hibernating in your loft. However, the best thing to do is to go up into your loft each year around February/March time. If there is an old wasps' nest then get rid of it – the queen will not be using this and it will only contain dead wasps. Next, look for a small ball, somewhere between the size of a ping-pong and a tennis ball, that looks like it's made of papier-mâché. This will be the new nest and will contain the queen wasp and a few of her daughters. If you destroy this small nest you will have no problem later in the year.

Incidentally, during most of their lives wasps are meat-eaters and will help rid your garden of aphids, bluebottles and so on, but will also eat bees and butterflies. Towards the end of their life, (August/September) they develop a sweet tooth (other than the queens) and this is when we notice them most as they are drawn by the smell of sweet food. If you want to create a wasp trap using a jar, bait it with jam. Do not use honey or you will attract bees.

Rose Confetti

Q. Can you tell me how to make rose-petal confetti for my daughter's wedding in September?

JO, Oswaldkirk, Yorkshire

A. The following is a recipe for rose pot-pourri; for confetti, I suggest omitting any ingredients that you feel would be too strong.

Gather the petals of fully open, sweet-scented roses in dry weather. Spread on a clean surface or paper in an airy room with an open window, or in the still air under a verandah or shed. When dried crisp, place in layers in a jar or bowl, sprinkling between each a mixture of 25g (1oz) powered orris root, 12g (½oz) bay salt, 6g (¼oz) allspice, 6g (¼oz) mace, 6g (¼oz) cinnamon, a small piece of gum alibanum and a few drops of an essential oil, violet perhaps. You can also add a few dried leaves of scented herbs: thyme, marjoram, mint, sage, basil, tansy and lavender flowers.

Stir well, seal with cling film and leave for two to three weeks. For pot pourri, then fill containers with perforated lids. For confetti, gently sieve out any granules and use the petals/leaves/flowerheads.

Bird Droppings

Q. Can you tell me how to remove a bird's droppings from clean sheets that were drying on the line?

PK, Llandrindod Wells, Powys

A. Normal droppings should come out if you rewash the sheets, but for droppings with berries in them soak the stain in a solution of one part 20-vol hydrogen peroxide to six parts cold water. On white fabrics, a diluted bleach can be used.

Don't Cry over Creosote

Q. Do you know how I could remove some creosote that I spilled in the boot of my jeep? The stain is bad and the smell overpowering!

DA, Knowle, West Midlands

A. Wipe over with white spirit and leave to soak for a while. Then scrub with a strong solution of detergent, such as Fairy Liquid, mixed with a little very hot water. The treatment may need to be repeated for complete success.

A Simple Solution

Q. I have a new carpet and a very old dog. When I left the dog at home one afternoon it had had an accident on the carpet. I am having trouble removing the stain and wonder if you can suggest anything that might help?

BR, Portsmouth, Hants

A. The best thing I have found for removing stains and odours, new and old, is a product called Simple Solution which is effective on urine, blood, vomit, faeces, mildew and anything organic. It is safe to use on carpets, upholstery, curtains, clothing and bedding – anything that is water-safe and colour-fast (test a small area to check). It is a non-toxic, bacterial enzyme formulation that speeds up the biodegradation process and smells slightly of vanilla.

If you have already tried to remove the stain with detergent you should rinse the area with clean water first; then apply Simple Solution all over and leave for five to 10 minutes before blotting up with kitchen paper. I have found it best to wipe it over with a wet cloth afterwards. If the stain is stubborn, repeat the process, possibly leaving the solution on overnight covered with a damp cloth to stop it drying out. It is stocked by good pet shops and by the chains.

Reader's top tips

DOG ODOUR

A great way to remove dog odour from the car is to sprinkle the seats with bicarb; after 20 minutes vacuum away. A saucer of vinegar left overnight will remove any lingering smell. Placing a fabric conditioner sheet behind the driver's seat every three weeks prevents further odour developing.

Two cups of vinegar solution added to the final rinse when washing your dog reduces its odour generally without discomfort to the dog.

Kay Grant, Hereford

Reader's top tips

WET DOG

To dry your dog quickly and efficiently, rub with a towel and pop it into a T-shirt, with its legs down the arm holes. Buy the T-shirt in a charity shop, combining two good things.

C M McDermott, Whitworth, Lancashire

Cluster's Last Stand

Q. As autumn is on its way, can you tell me how to deter bluebottles from packing themselves into our wooden window frames to hibernate? Is there a substance which can be applied to discourage them?

ARD, North Lyth, Caithness

A. The flies you describe are more likely to be cluster flies. Bluebottles are normally attracted to nastier things like rotten meat and dustbins. Cluster flies are similar in appearance but are no risk to health. However, they often cause problems in buildings when attempting to hibernate. To get rid of them you will need to apply to the window frames an insecticidal smoke/fog or spray, obtainable from good hardware stores.

Reader's top tips

FLIES

To keep flies off the windows, add a little paraffin to the water used for washing the windows. It gives a clear brilliant polish as well.

Pauline Watchorn, Bangor-on-Dee, Wrexham

Larder for Life

Q. We are planning to build a traditional larder in our house. It will have a stone floor and slate shelves. Can you tell me how to construct the inner walls, how to ensure there is ventilation and how we can prevent damp getting in?

DNM, Milton Keynes, Bucks

A. You should build the internal walls with air bricks and then plaster over them. This should avoid the need for damp-proofing. Incorporate an air vent in the outside wall and cover it with perforated zinc which can be bought at hardware shops.

Reader's top tips

SALT

Throw a handful of salt on the fire to keep your chimney clean.

Peter Olde, Kirkbymoorside, Yorkshire

Working on a Full Tank

Q. We have moved into a house that has a septic tank. Will brighteners, bleaches and enzymes in washing powers have any effect on the tank?

IG, Gargunnock, Stirlingshire

A. All active ingredients in soap and detergents are biodegradable by law and are safe for septic tanks in normal use but you should not dispose of anything in large quantities into the tank.

Do not pour any fats, oils or heavy grease down the drain. This also applies to paints, solvents, motor oils, garden chemicals and pesticides. Wash dishes in the dishwasher whenever possible as it converts fats into soap. You should use boiling water or rods instead of caustic soda to unblock a drain.

As the owner of a property with a septic tank you have a legal responsibility to ensure that it functions properly. Make sure that a dishwasher or washing machine is connected to a foul sewer or septic tank and not to a surface drain.

A comprehensive list of Dos and Don'ts is available from The Soap and Detergent Industry Association, 3/5 Clair Road, Haywards Heath, West Sussex, RH16 3DP, tel 01444 450884.

Oily Flags

Q. Have you any advice as to a method of removing a chainsaw oil stain from stone flags?

JP, Wiltshire

A. A number of people in the oil industry suggest that you should cover the stain with a fairly strong solution of detergent and leave it for half a day. Spray the detergent off with clean water, then cover the area with sand and shuffle around on it so that the sand acts as a mild abrasive. This will get rid of much of the stain but is unlikely to clear it completely. Once dry, you could use a sealant on the flags to prevent further staining.

Blotting Off Oil

Q. Very irritatingly, I have managed to stain my Norfolk jacket with gun oil. Can you suggest a way to remove it?

HJC, Oxon

A. Place some blotting paper over the stain and then press with a hot iron. The heat should loosen the oil for the blotting paper to soak up. You may have to repeat this treatment.

Reader's top tips

BOOTS

If your hunting boots are a bit tight, pull nylon pop socks up over your breeches.

Francesca Roy, London

Hard Work, Soft Hands

Q. Since I spend much of my time riding or working in the garden, I get through a lot of hand cream. Is it possible to make it myself?

E H-J, Buckinghamshire

A. Try the following. Put six dessert spoons of grated white beeswax, eight of sweet almond oil and eight of coconut oil into a basin over a pan of hot water. Melt and blend gently. Stir in 12 dessert spoons of glycerine, a drop at a time. Take off the heat, add six drops of lavender oil and stir until creamy. Put into pots and seal.

Reader's top tips

MUD

To restore mud-spattered stocks and breeches to sparkling whiteness, soak them in Napisan, available from supermarkets and chemists.

Philippa Cadogan, Frome, Somerset

Reader's top tips

LEATHER JACKETS

For applying cream to Barbour and leather jackets use an old shaving brush. It uses a tenth of the cream and takes a tenth of the time.

Sam Clough, Nelson, Lancashire

Sparkling Crystal

Q. Is there a way to make lead crystal glasses which are too delicate to go into the dishwasher sparkle?

LW, Loughborough

A. Clean using ordinary washing-up liquid in water no more than hand-hot. Rinse twice, first in clean warm water and then in warm water with a little methylated spirits or white-wine vinegar added. Dry and then polish the glass by holding a soft, lint free cloth in one hand and rotating the glass against it.

A Gilt-Edged Question

Q. Can you tell me how to clean my gilt picture frames, which are somewhat old, safely?

PT, London

A. The gold leaf used is extremely thin and therefore fragile. Added to this is the fact that there are two main kinds of gilt: oil-based and water-based. If the gilt is burnished then it will be water-based and if any of it has worn or been stripped away you will see a red colour coming through. If the gilt is matt it will probably be oil-based and worn or stripped areas would show through as a yellowy-ochre colour.

Any liquid cleaner, spirit or water-based, would damage either type of gilt and therefore the only absolutely safe method of cleaning is to wipe with a dry lint-free cloth such as silk.

As Clear as Crystal

Q. How can I remove whitish stains that look like lime scale from inside a decanter? Methods already tried without success include lead shot, coarse sand, lime scale remover and vinegar.

GLC, Goring-on-Thames

A. Dissolve some dishwasher powder in hot water and leave until luke-warm. Fill the decanter with this solution and stand for about three days, shaking occasionally. This will gradually loosen the lime scale from the glass and a bottle brush ought to finish off the job. You may have to repeat this process once or twice.

.... *Reader's top tips* ....

BABY WIPES

Baby wipes, available from any chemist or supermarket, make brilliant carpet stain removers. They are particularly good for removing blood.

Dee Murray, Beaulieu, Hampshire

Time Will Tell

Q. I have an old clock which has stopped, probably due to dirt and neglect. Is there anything I can do myself to get it going again as it is too large and heavy to take to a clock-mender.

ST, Devon

A. If it is simply a question of the clock being dirty, put a rag soaked in paraffin on a saucer in the bottom of the clock and wait. The vapour from the paraffin gradually loosens the dirt and the clock should start to work again. You may well have to be patient for up to a month or two before noticing any effects.

Coffee to Go

Q. Can you tell me how to remove an unsightly coffee stain from my lambswool jumper?

CN, Surrey

A. If the stain is recent moisten it and sponge with a solution of borax 15g to 250ml (½oz to ½ pint of tepid water); rinse and wash with a cold water woollen detergent.

Ageing Brass

Q. I need to replace some handles on an old chest of drawers but new brass will be very bright and obvious compared to the originals. Have you any suggestions?

PJE, Cumbria

A. Take your new brass handles and if they have been lacquered, remove this with paint-stripper. Place in a jam jar with a small pot of ammonia. The fumes will produce a 'worn' appearance on the surface of the brass.

The length of time to exposure will depend upon the effect you are seeking, but about 10 hours should suffice. Be careful not to expose them for too long or you may find the brass becomes damaged or will even disintegrate if it is very thin.

Reader's top tips

BRASS

Rather than spending a fortune on expensive cleaners to do the job, buff up brass to a nice shine with ketchup.

Mrs B Andrews, Oxon

Reader's top tips

YEAST

Yeast keeps longer if stored in the fridge and can last up to a year if left in the freezer.

Jenny Rolestand, London

Get it off your Chest

Q. I recently purchased at auction an old oak chest which looks rather dull and grubby. Can you tell me how to clean it up without doing any damage?

EK, Cornwall

A. Your chest's dirty appearance has probably been caused by a build-up of linseed oil and/or beeswax polish which has absorbed a lot of dirt and dust over the years. Much of this can be removed if you rub it down with a soft cloth using equal parts of raw linseed oil, vinegar and turpentine with ¼ part of methylated spirits, mixed together and shaken well.

To smooth off any roughness or particularly sticky patches, use fine steel wool. Then wipe it down using a soft cloth moistened with turpentine, and leave to dry. Vigorously rub in linseed oil daily for three to four weeks to give a very tough finish able to withstand damp and normal household damage.

.... *Reader's top tips* ....

TIGHT JAR LIDS

To open tight jar lids, put an elastic band around the top to give extra grip.

Helen Bedford, York

Cold Fire

Q. In my cottage in Gloucestershire I have a large, open fireplace. However, it is very disappointing because virtually all the heat seems to go up the chimney and not into the room. Can you suggest a remedy?

MK, Berkshire

A. The problem lies in the design of the chimney. Fireplaces which are cavernous with a tall, straight chimney are inefficient. It is the 'bent-knee' shaped fireplaces which give out the most heat. The only way to increase the warmth in your room would be to alter the chimney. You will need to seek advice from local stone masons and dealers in fireplaces. Rather an expensive solution, unfortunately.

Reader's top tips

FIRELIGHTER

To make environmentally friendly firelighters simply dry the peel of oranges or other citrus fruit on the Aga or in the airing cupboard. It's a clean and brilliant way to kindle or revive a fire.

Revd Roger Burt, East Coker, Somerset

Reader's top tips

OLD CANDLES

Old candles, particularly large ones, make ideal firelighters. Place one in a grate with some paper and a little kindling and it will produce a quick and easy fire.

Mrs R Drayton, Whepstead, Suffolk

Leaky Lead

Q. We consider our original leaded windows an attractive feature of our house, but unfortunately they let the rain in. Is there any way that we can repair them without having to resort to unsightly modern replacements?

TD-C, Essex

A. Over time, the leading between the panes of windows becomes a little loose, owing to differences in the expansion and contraction between the glass and the metal. First ensure that the panes are dry, then run a thin thread of plastic putty between the lead and the glass panes. It requires deftness, but it should be possible to ease the lead at the edge a little away from the glass in order to put in the putty, and then press the lead up again afterwards. The plastic putty will remain elastic, providing a good weatherproof seal.

Greasy Arms

Q. My fireside chairs are spoilt by the wooden arms, where one holds them, being dull and greasy. This will not polish off. I also have the same problem on part of my oak banister rail.

FW, North Yorkshire

A. It appears that the wooden arms of your chairs have probably become dull, sticky and greasy due to a build-up of varnish, wood finish, wax or oily polish, along with long handling.

A suggested treatment is to soften it up by applying a paint stripper, and then clean it off with a scraper or steel wool. Wash down with warm, soapy water, dry completely and then smooth with fine glass-paper, rubbing in the direction of the grain. The newly exposed surface can then be stained and repolished or covered with a polyurethane varnish.

If the wood has been French-polished, rub down with methylated spirit, but this would be ineffective on varnish. The alternative is to pay for a skilled craftsman to do the work.

Forget Elbow Grease

Q. Is there an easy way of cleaning my ornate silver bowl? I can no longer get hold of Goddard's Plate Powder and would like to know if there is an alternative.

JS, Suffolk

A. An effective and easy way of cleaning silverware is to collect milk bottle tops which you place in a bowl with a teaspoon of washing soda. Place the silver in the bowl so that it is touching the bottle tops and then cover the lot with boiling water. Leave for a few minutes until the silver looks clean. Take out and rinse.

Dry with a soft cloth and you should have a gleaming bowl. It is important not to leave the silver soaking for too long as the process starts to reverse itself.

Reader's top tips

PANS

To keep aluminium pans clean boil up water with a sliver of lemon peel for five minutes and existing stains will disappear.

Caroline Scott, Lamington, Lanarkshire

Reader's top tips

FAT USE

If you have goose flat left over from Christmas lunch it makes an excellent hoof oil and can be used over a horse's loins when being roughed off to prevent rain-scald.

Sarah Watts, Leicestershire

Anti-Ant Action

Q. How can I stop small, black ants from invading the house, floors and cupboards without using dangerous poisons?

DF, Surrey

A. An old fashioned 'safe' remedy is to mix together equal parts (by bulk) of powdered borax and icing sugar. Sprinkle the mixture where the ants are active, such as thresholds of doorways and cracks in the walls. Trace the ants back to their nest and dust over their nesting area and trails.

Spring Clean

Q. My oak garden furniture looks grey-green and dirty from being out of doors too long. How can I best clean it?

CD, Shropshire

A. Scrub with a solution of domestic bleach and then sponge down with clear water. When dry, smooth by rubbing down with sandpaper. Brush clear of wood dust and apply a preservative wood stain. Finally, give the furniture a coat of a weather-resistant polyurethane varnish.

Reader's top tips

WARTS

Tap a slice of garlic regularly over a stubborn wart to get rid of it.

John Hedley, by e-mail

Old Tiger

Q. My grandfather has left me a rather dirty, old, bedraggled, stuffed tiger's head. Can you recommend the best way to clean it?

AC, Northumberland

A. As long as the hair of the tiger's head and skin is still firmly anchored and the skin itself has suffered no deterioration, you can best clean the head by first removing all loose dust and detritus, carefully lifting it with a vacuum cleaner fitted with a small nozzle.

The fur can be further cleaned with a dry powder shampoo applied to the fur and then removed with the vacuum cleaner; or with a sudsy solution of a detergent suitable for wool (such as Stergene or Dreft) applied with a plastic sponge, rinsed off with clear, soft water, and then dried in the shade on a warm day or with a hair dryer.

The eyes and teeth can be wiped with a damp cloth dipped in detergent if necessary. There is no need for fresh preservative treatment but make sure that the head is dry before re-hanging.

You may need to watch out for moth and insect activity in the warmer months, but the application of a household insecticide around the base should prevent this.

Reader's top tips

HICCUPS

Cure for hiccups: forget all the nonsense about drinking water from the wrong side of the cup; one certain cure is to drink a teaspoon of vinegar.

Mr Williams, Llewesog, North Wales

Beetroot-Handed

Q. How can one get rid of vegetable stains from one's fingers?

JC, Cheshire

A. Rapid action is usually advisable with any type of stain. Vegetable stains can be removed from the fingers by soaking them for a few minutes in warm water to which a little lemon juice has been added. About a teaspoonful of lemon juice to 600ml (1 pint) of water should be sufficient. After soaking, the staining should easily rub off. An alternative method is to rub the stains directly with the skin of lemon or banana. After cleansing, the hands should be moisturised with a skin lotion.

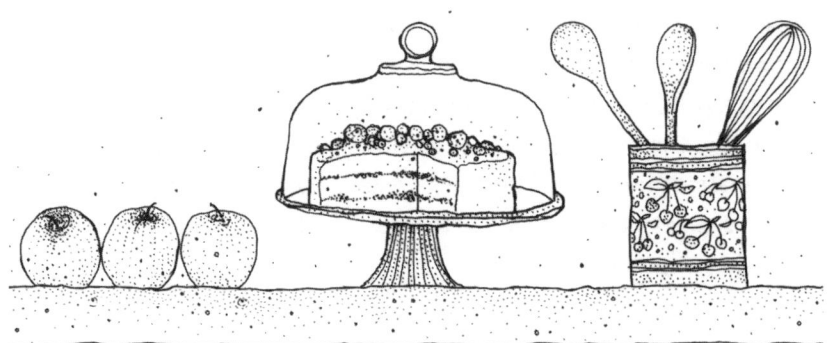

Food

Pigeon Pâté

Q. We seem to have an excess of pigeon and I have tried many different recipes. I would like to make a pigeon pâté but cannot find a recipe. Can you help?

EWC, Deddington, Oxon

A. This is from *The River Cottage Meat Book* by Hugh Fearnley-Whittingstall (Hodder & Stoughton).

Heat 25g (1oz) butter and one tbsp of olive oil in a frying pan, add a chopped onion and a large clove of chopped garlic. Fry until soft. Remove from the pan and add another 25g (1oz) butter and tbsp of olive oil. Turn up the heat and quickly fry the meat of six pigeon, plus two or three pigeon or chicken livers if you have them, until browned. Remove from the pan and place in a food processor. Quickly deglaze the frying pan with a small glass of port and tip this into the food processor along with an egg, 100g (4oz) sausage meat, one tsp redcurrant jelly, a sprig of thyme and a pinch of ground mace, and season with salt and pepper. Process until fine but with some texture. Line a dish with stretched streaky bacon, rind removed, leaving enough hanging over the sides to cover the pâté. Place the mixture in the dish and fold over the loose bacon. Cover with a double layer of greaseproof paper secured with string. Cook in a bain-marie at 180° for about 1½ hours. The pâté is ready when it starts to shrink away from the edge of the dish. Allow to cool. The flavour will improve if it is left in the fridge for a few days.

Pukka Pheasant

Q. My husband has completed his first season as a full gun on a shoot and consequently our freezer is full of pheasants. I was put off eating pheasant by friends preparing and cooking it extremely badly and haven't touched it since. I am now under pressure from my children and husband to roast them for Sunday lunch. I am at a loss, so many recipe books seem to differ. Can you help?

EE, by e-mail

A. *The Field's* cookery correspondent, Mike Robinson, has a simple and effective recipe for roasting pheasants in his book *Wild Flavours* (published by Cassell Illustrated). The book will also instruct you on how to make the perfect gravy which includes a tablespoon of tomato ketchup – to complement the pheasant. The basic recipe for roasting a brace of pheasants is quite simple. Preheat the oven to 160°. Place a lemon and a sprig of rosemary in the cavity of each bird, rub with a dessertspoonful of fat and place breast-side down in a roasting pan. Cover with foil and roast for 40 minutes. Increase the oven temperature to 200° and remove the birds. Turn them over and rub the breasts with another dessertspoonful of fat, sprinkle with more sprigs of fresh thyme and lay four rashers of streaky bacon over each breast. Return to the oven and roast, uncovered, for a further 20 to 25 minutes. When cooked, remove the birds from the oven and rest for 10 minutes. Make sure you drain off the fat from the roasting pan, leaving the juices behind so you can use them for gravy.

Carry on Carving

Q. Johnny Scott's article 'Carving through History' in *The Field* reminded me of my father carving all manner of birds and beasts with aplomb every Sunday. I would like to continue in his footsteps. Is there a book you can recommend that will help me in my pursuit? Can you also tell me where I can find a traditional bone-handled Sheffield steel carving set.

AJ, by e-mail

A. Johnny Scott and Clarissa Dickson Wright produced a book called *Sunday Roast: The Complete Guide to Cooking and Carving*, which is available at most good bookshops. It is full of useful information and advice on carving techniques to ensure your roast is correctly carved rather than hacked. Mike Robinson, who is *The Field's* cookery writer, runs a carving course for groups of eight at his cookery school in Berkshire. For further details visit www.gamecookeryschool.co.uk.

A stag-handled carver set can be bought from William Turner Master Cutlers, Sheffield. The set includes a carving-knife, carving-fork and carving-steel and the blades are forged. Call 0845 6710071 or visit www. williamturnersheffield.com

Freezing Fish

Q. I read with interest Adrian Dangar's piece in *The Field* 'A Smoky Business'. He said that it is better to gut the fish immediately on the riverbank prior to smoking. Does this apply if the fish is to be frozen before smoking? I have heard that frozen fish is not suitable, is this correct?

AN, by e-mail

A. Frozen fish can be used for smoking but it must be frozen straight after it is caught. Ideally a salmon should be frozen with its head on and guts intact; trout should be gutted and the blood channel along the spine scraped out and cleaned; a fish such as eel must be gutted as soon as possible as its guts quickly taint the flesh. Its single kidney must also be removed as it will render the finished product inedible. It is important to protect the fish from freezer burn by wrapping it in silver foil and brown paper which works better than plastic freezer bags. However, the thawing process can wash away some of the fish's natural oils.

Baked Beans

Q. Every year I get a quantity of broad beans that go 'over the hill' for eating fresh, young and tender. In Spain I believe they turn these mature beans into *habas fritas*, a type of snack. Can you find a recipe?

JR, Sussex

A. *Habas fritas*, in their simplest form, are just fried or roasted beans which are seasoned with salt or chilli flakes. They can also be cooked with onions and garlic. Firstly, pod the broad beans and remove the thick outer skin. Ideally leave to dry for an hour or so in the sun, the bottom of an Aga or warm oven. Heat some oil in a deep-fat fryer until it browns a cube of bread quickly, then gently lower the beans into the fat and fry them until they're crisp. Drain on kitchen towel and season with salt, pepper or chilli flakes. Alternatively, toss the peeled broad beans in oil and bake in a hot oven for 15 to 20 minutes until golden, and season. If using onions, sauté them in olive oil, add a thinly sliced clove of garlic and the broad beans, sprinkle with salt and cook until tender.

The Gravy Game

Q. I often find my gravy lacks flavour and I have been told that a pinch of coffee is a good enhancer for beef. Is there something that works well in gravy for game and chicken?

AML, Wootton, Oxford

A. For game, add tomato ketchup to enrich the gravy and give it some sweetness. Add the ketchup after you have worked the flour into the juices left by the meat and then continue as usual adding wine or stock as appropriate. A pinch of cocoa powder also works well with game. Soy sauce complements chicken gravy and gives it a depth of colour often lacking. The soy sauce can either be added to the pan before cooking or during the process. It is also a good addition to pork gravy while Worcestershire sauce goes with lamb. For sweetness a dash of honey blends nicely with pork and redcurrant jelly works well with most meats.

All flavourings should be added sparingly to ensure the gravy is not too highly flavoured – they are there to boost, not dominate. Juices still ooze from a joint as it rests and can be added to the gravy before serving.

Reader's top tips

GRAVY

To save the hassle of making gravy at the last minute make it in advance and put it in a heated thermos until needed.

P Henley, Cliburn, Cumbria

Syllabub Recipe

Q. I am trying to find a good, alcoholic, old-fashioned lemon syllabub recipe. Do you know of one?

MHW, Harrogate, Yorkshire

A. This is a good, gutsy recipe that has been around for many years. Thinly pare the rind from one lemon, place in a basin and pour over six tablespoons of cream or sweet oloroso sherry and two tablespoons of brandy. Squeeze the juice from the lemon, add to the bowl then cover and leave for a minimum of six hours, preferably overnight. Strain into a clean bowl, add 75g (3oz) of caster sugar and stir until dissolved. Add just under 300ml (½ pint) of double cream and whisk until the mixture stands in soft peaks. Place in glasses and chill until ready to serve to between six and eight people depending on the size of glass.

Batter those Elders

Q. Please could you let me have a recipe for elderflower fritters along the lines of courgette flower fritters that we had during the summer in Tuscany, which were delicious?

SF, Cambridge

A. This recipe uses oo flour, an Italian wheat flour which has a low extraction rate and ash content and also has a low protein content. It's the best flour for making pizza dough.

Ideally, the elderflowers should be picked in the morning after the sun has warmed them. Rather than washing them, shake the flowers carefully to remove small insects. For the batter you require 450g (1lb) oo flour, 25g (1oz) fresh yeast, 4 tablespoons caster sugar, a pinch of salt, 330ml (12fl oz) lager and some sparkling mineral water.

Place the flour in a large mixing bowl, add the yeast, sugar and salt and mix together. Make a well in the centre and pour in the lager and gradually whisk in the flour. Add as much sparkling water as required to form a loose batter the consistency of thickish double cream. Cover and leave in a warm place for 30 to 40 minutes to allow the yeast to activate. After this time a layer of foam will have formed on top. Preheat some sunflower oil in a deep fat fryer to 180°C. Dip the flowers into the foam layer of the batter and then place in the hot oil and fry for a minute or two until lightly golden and crisp. Drain on kitchen paper and dredge with caster sugar.

It's great served hot with vanilla ice-cream.

Storing Salami

Q. It's a real joy to be able to buy a large selection of salami on the market, but I find I am given different advice on the best way to store it. Can you help as I plan to give whole salamis as Christmas presents this year and would like to send correct storage advice with them.

GL, by e-mail

Q. As a cured meat salami can keep for months. The best way to store any cured meat is by hanging it in a cool and ventilated place (approximately 10°C to 15°C) where it will continue to mature. If this is not possible, then place in the fridge.

Salami is best eaten as soon as it is cut and you should remove only enough skin to access the quantity of salami you require. Without the skin, it won't last even if stored in the fridge.

Once cut, the salami should be covered tightly with cling film around the cut surface and placed in the fridge. You may notice that the cut end of the salami discolours – this is due to slight oxidation. The salt may also have started to crystallise on the end surface, which may alter the taste slightly, but it will just be the end piece that is affected and the remainder of the salami will be fine.

Scented Sugar

Q. Last year I dusted my mince pies with vanilla sugar, which I had made myself. Earlier this year I read an article saying that lavender sugar was also good, but I can't find any information on the correct quantities. I assume you can use dried lavender.

IL, Tackley, Oxfordshire

A. Dried or fresh lavender leaves can be mixed with caster sugar to give a delicate flavour, which can be used for sprinkling on cakes and using in puddings.

For one cup of sugar use either two tablespoons of dried lavender or four tablespoons of fresh. Place in a tight-lidded container in a warm place for one or two weeks, shaking occasionally to distribute the lavender among the sugar. Sift the sugar to remove the lavender heads and store the sugar in an airtight container.

In a Pickle about Walnuts

Q. When do I pick walnuts to pickle them and how do I pickle them? It will be my first crop from two young trees that are six or seven years old and 12ft high.

TH, Thirsk, Yorkshire

A. The immature green fruit required for pickling needs to be harvested in the summer before the shell has formed. Check for the readiness with a pin: stick it in the end where the flower was and if the shell has started to form it will be about a quarter of an inch in.

For 2kg (4½ lb) pickled walnuts you require enough water to cover the nuts, 225g (8oz) salt, 1 litre (1¾ pints) malt vinegar, 500g (1lb 2oz) brown sugar, 1 tsp allspice, 1 tsp cloves, ½ tsp cinnamon, ½ tsp black peppercorns and 1 tbsp fresh grated ginger. Prick the walnuts with a fork and cover with water and the salt. Leave for a week, then drain and renew with a fresh brine solution for another week. Drain the walnuts and lay out on trays in a dry, airy place. After a few days they will have turned black. Combine the remaining ingredients in a saucepan. Bring them to the boil, add the walnuts and simmer for 15 minutes. Cool and spoon the nuts into large jars and cover with the liquid. They should last for years.

Harvest the matured nuts when the protective green hull containing the brown nut splits. A proverb, 'A dog, a wife and a walnut tree; the more you beat them the better they be,' refers to the method used to fetch down the fruit and to break the long shoots to encourage the production of short fruit spurs.

From the Archives

The following appeared in *The Field* in September 1951

PICKLING ONIONS

Q. How can one prepare onions for pickling without shedding tears over them?

SJC

A. To prepare pickling onions without shedding tears over them, the simplest plan is to peel them under water, in a bowl large enough to accommodate your hands and the peeling knife. An old method, sworn to be efficacious by old-time Lancashire wives, is to have a piece of well-toasted bread crust in your mouth (like a cigar) while peeling them! You may find this piece of resuscitated old wives' lore worth trying. But the proper way to prepare small onions for pickling is to soak them unpeeled in brine (450g (1lb) salt to 2.25 litres (½ gallon water)) for 12 hours; then peel, and cover with fresh brine for 24 hours, rinse and drain well and pack in vinegar in the usual way.

Bergamot Tea

Q. I have grown the herb bergamot with the intention of using it to strengthen the flavour of my Earl Grey tea. Can you tell me how I go about infusing it with the commercial blend?

RP, by e-mail

A. The bergamot herb is not related to the bergamot orange, the peel of which is used to make the oil used in Earl Grey tea. Bergamot is a handsome perennial ideally planted in autumn or spring. It provides a good flow of flowers all summer.

Bergamot has an array of uses, culinary, medicinal and cosmetic. In cooking the leaves can give an Earl Grey flavour to China tea, be used in salads, for garnishes, in cheeses and tea. To make fresh tea, pour 600ml (1 pint) of water over approximately 25g (1oz) of bergamot leaves (for a single cup place four fresh or dried leaves in a cup and add boiling water). The tea is relaxing and can relieve nausea. The leaves also make an effective vapour treatment for the relief of catarrh and throat infections. Pour boiling water on to a large handful of leaves in a bowl and inhale the vapour.

Oast (not Oat) Cakes

Q. I am interested to know what oast cakes are and how to make them. Would you have a recipe?

JM, Martock, Somerset

A. Oasts are the buildings in which hops are dried. The cakes were originally made by the casual workforce of hop-pickers to eat as a snack in the hop gardens of Kent. The dough was made early in the day and then divided into small balls and fried over a campfire for the afternoon break. The pickers shallow-fried them in lard, but they can be deep-fried.

To serve six, you need 450g (1lb) plain flour, ½ tsp salt, 110g (¼lb) lard, diced, 110g (¼lb) currants, four tbsp each of beer and water, 50g (2oz) sugar, lard or vegetable oil for frying and caster sugar for coating. Sift the flour with the salt into a mixing bowl, add the lard and rub in until the mixture resembles fine breadcrumbs. Stir in the currants and mix to a stiff dough with the beer and water. Heat the lard in a frying-pan and cook until golden brown; alternatively, deep-fry in oil. Drain quickly on a piece of kitchen towel, roll in caster sugar and serve immediately.

Mincemeat Recipe

Q. I have not been able to find recipe for mincemeat that we truly enjoy and wonder if you can help.

WP, Framlingham, Suffolk

Q. This is a simple recipe and one with its roots firmly in the past. The exclusion of nuts and suet makes this appealing to many.

Place 450g (1lb) peeled and minced cooking apples, 450g (1lb) soft brown sugar, 450g (1lb) seeded raisins, 450g (1lb) currants, 225g (½lb) sultanas, 225g (½lb) finely chopped mixed peel (predominately lemon and lime), a whole, grated nutmeg, 1 tsp mixed spice and 1 tsp ground ginger in a large mixing bowl.

Add 450g (1lb) melted butter and the grated rind and juice of one lemon or orange. Stir thoroughly. At this point its appearance is very sloppy, but that is how it should be. Add 110ml (4fl oz) brandy and stir again. Leave for 24 hours and then decant into sterilised jars, cover and keep in a cool, dark place.

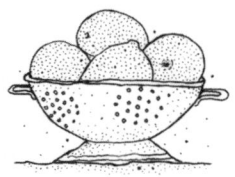

Wild Garlic

Q. Wild garlic grows in abundance in the hedgerows, woods and road-side verges in our area. Does it have any medicinal purposes and can I cook with it?

DJH, Cornwall

A. Wild garlic, *Allium ursinum,* is prolific throughout Britain, especially in the moist soil and semi-shade of woodlands. It is also known as ramsons, from the Anglo-Saxon word 'hramsa' meaning rank, because it was believed to taint the milk of cattle grazing on it.

This tasty plant has been used in herbal medicine for centuries. It is reputed to improve a range of conditions including high blood pressure, high cholesterol, indigestion, eczema, asthma and acne. It has known antibacterial properties and was written about in old English rhymes: 'Eat leeks in Lide [March] and ramsons in May, and all the year after physicians may play.'

Wild garlic has many culinary uses. The long, flat leaves have a subtler flavour than the normal cultivated garlic and are delicious raw or lightly cooked. They are great in sandwiches, used as a garnish for soups, scattered over omelettes or in scrambled eggs and stirred into stews. Use them in pesto instead of basil, in Béarnaise sauce instead of tarragon and in mushroom risotto instead of spinach.

Every part of the plant is edible, but digging up wild plants for the bulbs is frowned upon nowadays. The other beauty of wild garlic that it is far less offensive on one's breath than the cultivated variety.

Fruit Cake Fit for Family

Q. As a sailing family we consume an enormous amount of fruit cake and hot tea. I am trying to find a really good recipe for a fruit cake: one that is easy to make, not temperamental to bake, full of fruit, is moist and can be eaten immediately. I have tried many recipes but none has quite hit the spot with the panel of judges – my husband and children. Any suggestions?

RBM, Totnes, Devon

A. Fruit cake is very much a matter of personal taste, but I use a recipe from a village bakery in Northamptonshire. It had its heyday in Victorian times but it's been slightly adapted over the years. It produces a good, moist cake, is very simple to make and is ideal with whisky or tea after a hard day's sailing.

You will need: a 20cm (8in) cake tin (double-lined with brown paper to ensure the sides of the cake remain soft), 175g (6oz) margarine or butter, 175g (6oz) caster sugar, 3 large eggs, 110g (4oz) self-raising flour, 110g (4oz) plain flour, 225g (8oz) currants, 110g (4oz) sultanas, 110g (4oz) raisins and 50g (2oz) quartered glace cherries. The cherries should be rinsed in boiling water and cooled to prevent them sinking in the cake.

For a more fruity effect you can add 50g (2oz) chopped peel or 75g (3oz) dried fruit.

Preheat the oven to 250°F/130°C Gas Mark ½. Cream the margarine or butter and sugar together. Add the eggs one at a time with a tablespoon of flour, whisking after each one. Fold in the flour, fruit and cherries. Add enough milk to give it a soft consistency. Pour into the cake tin.

Bake for approximately 2½ hours but check after 1½ hours. If the top looks brown reduce the temperature to 225°F/110°C/Gas Mark ¼. Test with a skewer – the cake is cooked if the skewer is clean when removed. Cool in the tin. Eat immediately.

Flour-free Cake

Q. I have a friend coming to stay who is allergic to wheat. Can you suggest a recipe for a good cake that is not made with flour?

AK, Woking, Surrey

A. The following recipe is from my file of recipes collected over the years and was torn out of a magazine; I don't know which one or when. Whisk 6 egg whites until stiff and set aside. In another bowl, whisk the 6 egg yolks and 250g (9oz) caster sugar together but not to the stage where it is very pale and thick. Into this, gently fold the egg whites in three portions, followed each time by folding in 117g (4oz) ground almonds and a third of a teaspoon of baking powder, mixing until evenly incorporated. Divide the eventual mixture between two 20cm (8in) buttered cake tins and give them a couple of taps on the worktop to bring up any large air bubbles. Bake for 35 minutes in an oven preheated to 190C° (170C° in a fan oven)/Gas Mark 5, until the tops feel springy to the touch and the sides are shrinking away from the tin. Run a knife round the side of each cake and remove it from the tin. Leave them to cool on a wire cooling rack.

Sandwich the two sponges together with raspberry jam worked till it is smooth with some fresh raspberries (if available) gently stirred in. dust the top with icing sugar.

Lavender Aplenty

Q. We grow lots of lavender, which attracts bees and butterflies, but we have never tried using it in cooking. Can you suggest a simple recipe?

MG, Lymington, Hants

A. *The Lavender Cookbook* by Sharon Shipley is ideal when it comes to lavender for cooking. It gives recipes for use with spring, summer and autumn lavender. There is advice on cultivating for the kitchen and for harvesting and drying. Recipes range from the basics of lavender sugar, syrup, butter and bread, to the entrée grilled lavender halibut in banana leaves with tropical raspberry salsa, and the pudding lavender honey custard ice-cream.

Lavender ginger lemonade is perfect for a summer afternoon: in a processor, combine 1 cup sugar, 110g (4oz) crystallised ginger, 2 tbsp dried culinary Provence lavender buds and the grated zest of 2 lemons. Blend for 1 minute, or until the ginger is in small pieces. Transfer to a medium saucepan, add 2 cups water, bring to the boil and cook for 1 minute. Strain into a heatproof bowl; and discard the solids. When cold, combine the syrup in a pitcher with 4 cups water and half a cup of fresh lemon juice. Stir well. Add ice and stir to chill or serve in ice-filled glasses.

Plum Pudding

Q. Why is Christmas pudding often called plum pudding when it has no plums in it?

CW, Sproxton, Leics

A. It appears that it was originally a 14th century soupy porridge made by boiling beef and mutton with raisins, currants and spices, such as ginger, and was eaten as a fasting dish prior to the indulgence of Christmas. By the end of the 16th century it had evolved into a dessert pudding, having been thickened with eggs and breadcrumbs, and made more flavoursome with the addition of ale and/or spirits and dried fruit, particularly prunes – hence 'plum pudding'. The Puritans then removed it from the menu, banning it as a lewd custom 'unfit for God-fearing people'. It remained absent until George I, who was partial to it, re-established plum pudding as part of the Christmas feast in 1714.

By Victorian times, it had become similar to the pudding we enjoy today, although the plum element seems to have departed since most recipes call for 'mixed dried fruit', which we tend to interpret as raisins, currants and sultanas. It has become a tradition and been embroiled in superstitions along the way. It is believed one should begin making puddings on 'stir up Sunday', the 25th Sunday after Trinity/the Sunday before

Advent to allow time for them to mature; prepare with 13 ingredients to represent Christ and his Disciples; all members of the family to make a wish while taking a turn to stir and stirring from east to west in honour of the Three Kings; mixing in a silver coin to bring health, wealth and happiness to whoever finds it in their portion of pudding; and decorating before serving with a sprig of holly to represent Christ's crown of thorns.

Preserving Eggs

Q. Years ago, people preserved eggs using water-glass. My daughter has just started to keep hens. Can you still buy water-glass, and how is it used?

BL, Long Sutton, Somerset

A. Water-glass used to be widely available in household stores and village emporiums catering for farmers' wives and country people. It is still manufactured by various firms though is very difficult to find on the shelves. With luck, you might find a chemist or household shop in your area that is able to supply it.

Put your newly laid eggs in a bucket or ceramic crock and pour over a solution of one part water-glass to nine parts water, making sure the eggs are completely covered. Then put the lid on. Kept somewhere cool and with no disturbance they should keep a good six months. Another method is to grease the eggs using something such as lard: the eggs should be treated individually by placing a small dab of grease in the palm of your hand and carefully rolling each egg to coat it as evenly as possible. Then place them, pointed end downwards, in clean trays or boxes and store in a cool place. All these methods aim to keep air away from the eggs, thus delaying the natural aging process.

Turkish Delight

Q. I have a large family and we are all partial to Turkish delight. Perhaps it's me but the shop bought stuff doesn't seem to taste like it used to. Can you provide a recipe so that we could try making it ourselves?

JWC, Chesham, Bucks

A. The following recipe comes from Claudia Roden's *A Book of Middle Eastern Food*, published by Nelson. Dissolve 900g (2lb) sugar and the juice of half a lemon in 570ml (1 pint) of water, and bring to the boil. Mix 175g (6oz) cornflour with 275ml (½ pint) of water to make a smooth paste. Add this gradually to the hot syrup, off the heat, stirring constantly with a wooden spoon. Return to the heat for at least 30 minutes, stirring as often as you can, until the mixture thickens considerably and has lost its floury taste. Add ½tsp pulverised mastic pounded with a little granulated sugar. Stir in thoroughly and cook for a few minutes longer. Add a few drops of cochineal and 2tbsp rose water, stir well and cook for a further one or two minutes. Add 110g to 225g (¼lb to ½lb) chopped almonds or pistachios and mix well.

Pour the hot mixture about 3cm (1¼in) deep into a tray which has been dusted with cornflour.

Flatten with a knife and leave for 24 hours to set. It will need a further period of several days to dry out. When dry, cut into squares with a sharp knife and roll in sifted icing sugar. The Turkish delight will keep for a long time packed in a box. For a richer flavour, substitute a little grape juice for some of the water added to the cornflour.

Apples to Keep

Q. Can you please tell me the best way of storing apples through the winter? I always seem to end up with a lot of shrivelled ones.

JDM, Ashbourne, Derbyshire

A. Apples for storing that have been picked too early will shrivel. To check whether the apples are ready for picking, cut one in two and paint the flesh of one half with iodine. If it turns completely black leave them on the tree a while longer. If approximately a quarter turn brown, they are ready for storing. If three-quarters turns brown, then most of the starch has turned to sugar and they are ready for eating.

Pick the apples with stalks intact and put into polythene bags to keep the moisture in and stop any mould from spreading – leave slightly open so the apples can breathe. Store the apples in a cool shed or cellar and cover with straw or cardboard to help keep the temperature stable (avoid attics, which can be dry and warm). Check occasionally and remove any that have deteriorated.

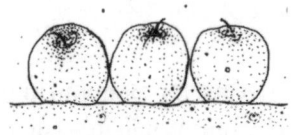

No More Peeling

Q. During the first two weeks of September I peeled and cored windfalls for chutney and the freezer until my hands were sore. There are still stacks on the trees that will be ready for picking towards the end of October and which I will put into store.

However, there will be too many cookers for ordinary use. Can you suggest any recipes that don't require peeling and coring as I cannot face doing any more?

CM, Giggleswick, N. Yorks

A. I suggest the following recipes. Apple Jelly by Prue Coats: wash 1.8kg (4lb) crab, cooking or windfall apples, remove any bad bits and cut up roughly. Do not peel or core. Put into a pan with 2.25 litres (4pt) water and cook until mushy. Place in a jelly bag, hang over a bowl and leave to drip overnight to extract all the pectin. Measure the liquid, pour into a pan and add 570g (1¼lb) granulated sugar to each 570ml (1 pint) of liquid. Place over a low heat and stir until all the sugar has dissolved; then turn up the heat and bring to a full, rolling boil, periodically skimming off any scum. Place a metal plate in the freezer and after 30 minutes put a few drops of the apple on to the plate. When it cools run your finger over it and if it wrinkles the jelly is ready to pot up. Warm your sterilised jam jars in a low oven and fill them right to the top.

Cover each with a square of cling film pulled tightly. As the jelly cools it will create a vacuum. When cold put on screw tops.

Mrs Beeton's Apple Butter: wash 3kg (6lb 11oz) crab, cooking or windfall apples and cut into chunks, discarding any bruised or damaged portions. Place in a preserving pan with 1 litre (1¾ pt) cider and bring to the boil, then lower the heat and simmer for about an hour or until the fruit is tender. Sieve into a bowl. Weigh the pulp, put into a clean pan and simmer until it thickens. Add three-quarters of the pulp's weight in sugar, 1tsp ground cloves and 1tsp ground cinnamon. Stir over a gentle heat until the sugar has dissolved, then boil steadily, stirring constantly, until no free liquid runs out when a small sample is cooled on a plate. Pot, cover at once and label. Makes 3.25kg (7lb 4 oz).

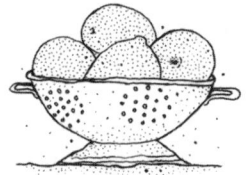

Sweet Weeds

Q. I have tried using dandelions from my garden in salads but they were rather tough and bitter. Can you tell me why this is, as they are often described as being edible?

LL, London

A. Young, healthy dandelions that have not caught so much as a whiff of weedkiller will be more succulent but will still taste bitter. On a dry day, I suggest you try loosely tying up the leaves of a young dandelion and covering them with a large pot, keeping them in darkness until the inner leaves whiten and become sweeter. Then blanch the leaves before adding to a salad. If all your dandelions are rather old and large, cut off the entire crown and a new flush of leaves will appear.

Sugared Petals

Q. How can I apply sugar-frosting to rose petals?

JA, Selsdon, Surrey

A. Collect 30 or so dry, fresh, soft rose petals and lay them out singly. Have ready a plate with a good amount of caster sugar on it. Then, whip an egg white together with 1tsp of rosewater. Dip one rose petal at a time into the egg white mixture, making sure it is entirely covered and then immediately dip into the sugar, pressing firmly to make sure you get a good layer of sugar all over. Transfer to a wire rack and leave to dry for an hour at least.

Sugared petals can be stored for up to a fortnight somewhere cool and dry. They lose their 'crunch' as soon as they become moist, so add to cakes and puddings at the last moment.

Pickled Ginger

Q. Please can you tell me how to make gari?

RR, Tring, Herts

A. Peel 225g (8oz) of fresh root ginger and slice as thinly as possible. Place in a bowl, cover with cold water and leave to soak for about half an hour. Drain and drop into a pan of boiling water. Bring back to the boil, drain again, transfer into a clean bowl, and leave to cool. Then sprinkle with sea salt.

Combine 250ml (8fl oz) of rice vinegar and 1tbsp of sugar in a saucepan, and stir over a gentle heat until the sugar dissolves. Pour this over the ginger, ensuring it is entirely submerged, cover and leave to marinate somewhere cool and dark for a minimum of two weeks. Then bottle, seal with a vinegar proof lid and keep in the fridge.

Gari is traditionally served with sushi but goes very well with other seafood and poultry. It can also be used on its own as a palate cleanser between courses.

Making No Bones About It

Q. Now that there is no problem with buying beef marrow bones, can you give a recipe for beef marrow toast?

LC, St Ives, Cambs

A. You need a marrow bone cut in lengths to get at the marrow; your butcher could do this quite easily.

Mix together 1tbsp parsley and 1tsp chopped shallot or spring onion, season with salt and pepper and add a squeeze of lemon juice. Put to one side.

Remove the marrow from the bone, cut it into small pieces and poach in a little salted boiling water for a minute only. Drain and toss the marrow in the parsley mixture, and immediately spread it on hot buttered toast. Squeeze a little lemon juice over the top and eat straightaway.

Marrons Glacés

Q. I adore chestnuts, and always use them for stuffing the turkey as well as roasting on the fire. This year I'd like to have a go at marrons glacés and would be grateful for a recipe.

JH-B, by e-mail

A. Prick the skins of 700g (1½lb) fresh chestnuts, drop into boiling water and boil for three to four minutes. Drain. When cool enough, peel and remove the dark skin. Place in a saucepan, cover with cold water, bring to the boil and simmer gently for eight to 10 minutes until tender. Drain. Make a syrup using 275ml (½ pint) cold water, 350g (12oz) caster sugar, 225g (8oz) powdered glucose and ½ tsp vanilla essence. Over a low heat, stir gently until the sugar and glucose have completely dissolved, then add the chestnuts and bring to the boil. Remove the pan, put the lid on and leave in a warm place for 48 hours. Drain. Make some fresh syrup, as above, using 150ml (¼ pint) cold water, 350g (12oz) caster sugar and ½tsp vanilla essence; then insert a sugar thermometer and boil until it reaches 120°C. Remove from the heat and add the chestnuts. Ensure they are fully coated in syrup before lifting on to a wire rack to drain and dry thoroughly. Store in an airtight container.

Hasty Pudding

Q. When as children we visited our granny, she often gave us something she called Hasty Pudding. Sadly she is no longer with us and there is no trace of the recipe; she must have kept it in her head. Do you know of a recipe?

RL, Cambridge

A. Your grandmother may have had her own version but I have found a recipe dated 1941. It is as follows: put 570ml (1 pint) of milk into a saucepan with a pinch of salt and bring to the boil. Gradually sprinkle in a sufficient quantity of plain flour to make a stiff batter, stirring and beating continuously. Boil for a minute or so to cook the flour and then take off the heat. Allow the batter to cool, add two beaten eggs, return to the heat and cook gently without allowing it to boil again. Turn the mixture into a dish with a few knobs of butter, a little sugar to taste, and serve with golden syrup or jam.

Oh Lardy!

Q. Some bakers still make lardy cakes. Do you have a recipe?

GC, Corby, Northants

A. You could try this old recipe I found. On a floured board, roll out 450g (1lb) of bread dough into an oblong shape. Mix 110g (4oz) of English lard with 50g (2oz) sugar, a little spice and a few currants and spread half of it on to the dough.

Fold over and dredge lightly with flour. Fold up, as for flaky pastry, and give the dough a half-turn. Repeat this using the other half of the lard mixture. Then repeat the following process, giving a dredging of flour.

Roll out to about ½in thickness, round off the corners and score the top with a knife. Put the dough into a warmed, greased and floured tin. Leave for 15 minutes, brush with a little warm milk and bake in a hot oven for 20 to 30 minutes until golden.

Gathering Nuts this Way

Q. My walnut trees are laden this year but how can I prise the nuts out of the husks? I have heard that they should be immersed in wet sand. Is this correct?

AE, Manningtree, Essex

A. Gather the walnuts when they are ripe and falling. Spread them out in a single layer to dry in a shed or somewhere similar for a few days. Using a stiff-bristled brush and water, remove every last bit of the husk, or put them in a tub with sand and water and scrub with a stiff-bristled broom. Spread them out on trays to dry again – in an area where there is a current of air.

When dry, they should be stored in boxes. Put a layer of sand at the bottom of a box then a layer of nuts and sprinkle with salt. Add another layer of sand but only just cover the nuts. Repeat until the box is full.

The salt prevents the nuts from shrivelling but as they will not keep for ever, do try and use them as soon as you can.

Biscuits from Land's End

Q. I haven't been to Cornwall for years but I remember those delicious spicy biscuits called Cornish fairings. I imagine they are still available in Cornwall but would like to try making them myself. Do you have a recipe?

RA, Radcliffe on Trent, Notts

A. Cream 110g (4oz) butter, 110g (4oz) caster sugar and 110ml (4fl oz) syrup together until light and fluffy. Make a soft dough by adding 225g (8oz) of sifted plain flour, two level teaspoons of baking powder, two level teaspoons of bicarbonate of soda, two level teaspoons of ground ginger and one level teaspoon of mixed spice.

Roll the dough into small balls and slightly flatten the top of each. Put them on to a well greased baking tray and bake in a pre-heated oven at

150°C/300°F/Gas Mark 2, for about 15 minutes. The biscuits spread out to form thin crispy circles so remember to leave plenty of room between them on the baking tray.

Flaming Dragons

Q. Some time ago I saw a recipe for the unusually named Flaming Snapdragon. I jotted it down on the back of an envelope but have since lost it. Do you know the recipe?

LT, Dowbridge, Lancs

A. This is a very simple dish made of dried fruits such as sultanas, figs apricots and so on, soaked in brandy for about 24 hours until they are nice and plump.

Gently heat the fruit and brandy in a saucepan. Pour into a warmed dish and set alight. Serve the Flaming Snapdragon with cream or ice cream as soon as the flames have died down.

Traditional Bangers

Q. Can you give me an old-fashioned recipe for making sausages?

TASC, Newquay

A. The following recipe comes from a very old copy of Mrs Beeton. Finely chop and mix together 450g (1lb) pork (both fat and lean but without skin or gristle), 450g (1lb) lean veal and 450g (1lb) beef suet.

Mix in 225g (8oz) breadcrumbs, the finely minced peel of half a lemon and one small nutmeg, grated. Add six washed and chopped sage leaves, 1tsp pepper, 2tsp salt, ½tsp savory and ½tsp marjoram and mix thoroughly. Put the meat into skins or form it into little cakes, but flour them before frying.

Pigeon Pâté

Q. Earlier this year you gave a good recipe for using up pheasants from the freezer. We have a similar problem: my husband shoots woodpigeon and we seem to use the breasts only. So the freezer is fully of pigeon legs. Could you suggest a recipe to use them up?

DBC, Surrey

A. Make pigeon pâté. The recipe comes from *Game Cookery* by Angela Humphreys, published by David & Charles.

Make a marinade of 150ml (¼pt) red wine, 1 chopped onion, 2tsp mixed herbs, 1 bay leaf and a pinch of nutmeg. Pour over 16 pigeon legs: cover and chill for two to three days. Put the pigeon legs and marinade, with 150ml (¼pt) stock, in a saucepan and simmer for 1 hour. When cool, remove 225g (8oz) of meat from the bones and mince finely. Mix with 225g (8oz) pork sausage meat, 1tsp mixed herbs, seasoning and enough of the strained stock to make a smooth mixture.

Place the pâté in a buttered ovenproof dish. Cover with a lid or foil and bake in a moderate oven, 180°C/350°F/Gas Mark 4/bottom right oven in a four door Aga, for 1½ hours. Chill overnight and serve on crisp-bread or toast.

Pheasant Pie

Q. At this time of year I have so many pheasants in the freezer there is no room for anything else. Can you suggest a good recipe for using them up?

RSJO, Newbury

A. The following recipe was sent in by Mrs Inis Compton of Hartpury, Gloucestershire for this very purpose.

Finely chop one large onion or six shallots. Peel, core and chop four dessert apples into very small pieces. Fry the onions and apples in a little oil and butter and cook until soft. Dice the meat from a roasted pheasant and add to the onion and apples along with a long shake of Worcester sauce. Add salt and pepper to taste and stir well.

Mix one dessertspoon of chicken gravy granules into half a cup of boiling water. Add to the mixture, stirring continuously until thickened. Remove from the heat and cool. Line a 20 or 23cm (8 or 9in) pastry dish with puff pastry and add the pheasant mixture. Top with a pastry lid and seal the sides. Cook for one hour at 400°F/200°C/Gas Mark 6 until golden brown. Serves six.

From the Archives

The following appeared in *The Field* in September 1952

SMOKING SALMON

Q. What is the method used to kipper or smoke salmon?

ECWH

A. The general method of kippering or smoking salmon is to scale the fresh fish, then split it down the back, removing the head and backbone except for about 7.5cm (3in) at the tail, and clean and dry it. Rub with a mixture of equal quantities salt and Jamaica pepper and leave for 24 hours. Then drain, rub well with salt 450g (1lb), brown sugar 75g (3oz) and saltpetre 25g (1oz) two or three times. Stand for two days and repeat the rubbing. Then stretch the fish on a wooden stick framework, and hang by the tail, in the sun or by a fire to dry off a little, and smoke in the woodsmoke from smouldering sawdust, juniper branches or turf, for at least three days.

This treatment can be modified according to the result desired, and the amount of smoking etc. determines how long the fish will keep. Under proper conditions, a well-kippered salmon should keep for two to three months or more.

Gentleman Relish It

Q. Patum Peperium, or Gentleman's Relish, is my favourite spread on hot buttered toast. Why does it have two trade names and is there a story behind the name Gentleman's Relish?

PJT, East Sussex

A. There is indeed a story. In 1828, John Osborn, an Englishman living in Paris, concocted this recipe using anchovies, butter, herbs and spices, as a delicacy specifically for spreading on toast. Because of its exceptional piquancy and intensity of flavour, he named it Patum Peperium; *patum*, Latin for paste or pâté and 'peperium', stemming from Latin and Greek meaning pepper – paste of peppers.

It became so popular in Paris that Osborn abandoned his provisions business and concentrated solely on this paste. Before his death in 1865, he revealed the recipe and method to his son Charles, and impressed upon him never to put the recipe in writing, never to allow any one employee to be involved in the whole process, and that the recipe was to be adhered to by each generation.

The business then transferred to a factory in Stoke Newington, London and the recipe was handed down from Charles Osborn to his sons, Harold and Newton. The paste became extremely popular among the aristocracy in London. When buying the paste, people would ask for, 'Patum Peperium. You know, the gentleman's relish', to such a degree that the Osborns decided to make it official and added it to their original name.

As there was no family left to continue the business, the Osborns sold the company to Elsenham Quality Foods in 1971. On the sale Harold revealed one part of the process and Newton the other. The recipe is still greatly guarded and ingredient X, which is the infusion of spices and herbs, is known only to a very few people and the method is still not known by any one person.

It is widely sold now in a variety of styrene, glass and porcelain pots, the porcelain ones being decorated with many different designs from shire horses to sporting scenes and vintage cars.

Edible Decorations

Q. I want to make some Lebkuchen to hang on the Christmas tree this year. Do you have a recipe?

A. The following recipe will make fairly light and crisp biscuits suitable for tree decorations.

Sift 110g (4oz) self-raising flour into a bowl and set to one side. Melt 40g (1½oz) runny honey and 40g (1½oz) soft brown sugar in a pan and bring to the boil. Remove from the heat and add 1tsp brandy and 50g (2oz) butter. Stir until the mixture is nice and smooth. Add a pinch each of cinnamon, ginger and ground nutmeg.

Fold into the flour to make a dough, roll out fairly thinly, about 5mm (¼in), and cut out using a heart-shaped pastry cutter. At the top of each biscuit, not too close to the edge, make a small hole to thread the string through. Place on a greased baking tray and bake at 180°C/350°F/Gas Mark 4 for 10 minutes until the biscuits are browned. Leave to cool and decorate with white icing. Store in an airtight tin.

Soft Fruit Surfeit

Q. Last year *Country Queries* advised how to use up excess raspberries by making ratafia. Have you any other suggestions for ways of using up soft fruits and enjoying them beyond the summer?

SAA, West Sussex

A. The following recipes are a great way to enjoy summer fruits out of season.

For an iced strawberry treat: purée 450g (1lb) of strawberries with a tablespoon of lemon juice. Transfer into a large mixing bowl and fold in 275ml (½ pint) of whipped double cream. In a separate bowl beat three egg whites until stiff, and add 175g (6oz) of sugar, a tablespoon at a time, beating thoroughly until really thick. Then fold into the strawberry and cream purée. Spoon into soufflé or individual dishes and freeze. Transfer to the fridge one hour before serving.

Try this recipe when there is a glut of raspberries: pick raspberries when just ripe. Put into a bowl, add an equal quantity of caster sugar, and fork together. Put into preserving jars up to the shoulder of the jar, top up to the rim with caster sugar and screw on the lid. Store in a cool dry place and they will keep for several months.

Easy Treats

Q. Do you know of any easy recipes for interesting sweets and nibbles?

EVW, Oxford

A. Firstly, can I recommend walnut bon-bons: make some honey marzipan by taking 100g (4oz) ground almonds plus 1tbsp thick honey and mixing them into a firm paste, adding a few drops of vanilla and almond essence. Add a few drops of green or yellow colouring if desired and work in smoothly. Then sandwich a small ball of the honey marzipan between two walnut halves using a little apricot jam.

Or try salted almonds: put shelled almonds into a bowl of boiling water. Leave them until they are cool enough to handle and then pop them out of their skins. Mix some salt and a little cayenne pepper together on some greaseproof paper and keep to hand. Take a small pan and melt enough butter to give about 1in in depth. Bring to the boil and throw in the blanched almonds all at once so that they brown equally. Take the almonds out and roll them in the salt mixture, shaking well until cool.

Finally, you could try duchesse nougat: take 25g (1oz) powdered gelatine, 200g (7oz) sugar, 275ml (½ pint) water, a stiffly beaten egg white, 200g (½lb) chopped blanched almonds and 2tsps vanilla essence. Place the gelatine, sugar and water in a saucepan and bring to the boil, stirring all the time. Continue boiling and stirring for eight minutes. Remove from the heat, cool slightly and then beat in the egg white, almonds and vanilla. Pour into a buttered, cornflour-dusted tin and leave to set. Then cut the nougat into neat squares.

Cakes and Ale

Q. Having baked a rich fruit cake, is there a way of storing it for use at a future date?

ML, Essex

A. Wrap the cake carefully in a cloth soaked in brandy or wine and then in foil to keep for a short time. For longer storage bury the alcohol-soaked cake in confectioner's sugar in an airtight tin and store in a cool place.

Sugar-Sweet Violets

Q. The crystallised violets used for decorating sweets are very expensive to buy. Is this something I could easily do myself?

RK, Salisbury

A. Put a spoonful of powdered gum Arabic in a small screw-top jar. Add rosewater until it just covers the powder and leave for a few days to dissolve. Paint freshly picked purple or white sweet violets ensuring the petals are completely covered, sprinkle with caster sugar and place on a wire rack somewhere warm. Once they are dry and crisp, keep in an airtight tin until required.

Digestible Digestives

Q. Digestive biscuits are easy to buy but I would like to try making them myself. Do you know of a good recipe?

MHF, London

A. The following will produce a biscuit which keeps very well and has a good, nutty flavour. Take 110g (4oz) oatmeal (medium cut), 110g (4oz) wholemeal flour, 10g (½oz) demerara sugar, 75g (3oz) butter, 10ml (½fl oz) milk, ½tsp bicarbonate of soda, a dash of lemon juice and a pinch of salt.

Mix together the oatmeal, flour, sugar, bicarbonate of soda, lemon juice and salt and rub in the butter to produce a crumbly consistency. Add the milk, mixing with a fork into a light dough. Roll out the dough to a thickness of about ⅛in on a floured surface, cut into circles and prick all over.

Cook in a preheated oven (180°C/350°F/Gas Mark 4) on greased baking trays until lightly browned – approximately 15 minutes. Remove from the oven and place on a cooling rack.

Venison Burgers

Q. Do you know of any recipes for venison burgers?

GW, France

A. The following recipe for venison cakes is quite delicious. Mix together 400g (1lb) finely minced venison, 50g (2oz) minced fatty pork or bacon, 25g (1oz) fresh breadcrumbs, 2 copped shallots, 1 teaspoon dried thyme, 1 pinch *Quatre Epices* and 1 beaten egg. Season with salt and ground black pepper. Taking a tablespoon as a time, roll in flour then flatten into cakes. Fry in a mixture of oil and butter and serve with sautéed potatoes and puréed chestnuts. Redcurrant jelly is a good accompaniment.

.... *Reader's top tips* ....

TOMATOES

A means of enjoying garden tomatoes into late fall; remove all the green tomatoes very early in October. Wrap them individually in newspaper, then store in a cool, dry place. The tomatoes will ripen slowly and taste like a fresh garden tomato.

R W Griffith, Summerland, Canada

Sugared and Spiced

Q. Can you suggest a way to dress up plain nuts and make them a little more interesting?

RCG, London

A. Try the following recipe. Take 100g (4oz) caster sugar, 1tsp cinnamon, ½tsp ground ginger, a pinch of ground nutmeg, ½tsp ground coriander, one egg white, and 50g (2oz) each of shelled walnuts, blanched almonds and shelled hazelnuts.

Mix together the sugar and spices in one bowl and beat the egg white in another. Coat each nut with the egg white and toss the sugar and spice mixture covering them completely. Place them on a lightly oiled baking tray and bake for 20 minutes at 350°F/180°C/Gas Mark 4. Then sprinkle the nuts with the remaining sugar and spice mixture and return to the oven for a further five minutes. Allow to cool and store in layers of greaseproof paper in an airtight tin.

Unsavoury Sand

Q. Often, when I have eaten mussels, they have been gritty. Can you suggest a good way of cleaning them and getting rid of the sand?

MJG, Hampshire

A. Buy your mussels the day before you want to use them and throw them, dirty, into a bucket. Add no water. Cover with coarse oatmeal or porridge oats and put the bucket into a dark place overnight. The mussels will open and stodge the oatmeal, thereby cleaning themselves and disposing of potentially dangerous impurities. In the morning pour the mussels into the sink and scrub them under plenty of cold running water. Then tug off the beards. When the cold water they are standing in is clear and clean, sort through and throw away any that are not tightly closed. The remaining mussels can then be cooked.

A Nettling Question

Q. My grandfather has often told me about war time deprivation forcing him to eat nettles. Are they really palatable, and if I want to try them, how should I prepare and cook them?

GP, Devon

A. Despite their ability to sting when they come into contact with the skin, nettles are indeed remarkably good to eat. It is best to gather spring shoots in the first flush of growth when they are young and tender, wearing stout gloves. They are less palatable when the foliage toughens.

Once crushed down, nettles lose their sting and can be put in to a salad or used in soup. As an infusion, nettles are said to be good as a blood-cleanser.

Another method of serving is to make 'nettle spinach', which makes a very good vegetable accompaniment to an evening meal. After washing the shoots, boil in slightly salted water until tender. Drain well and chop finely. Re-heat them and season liberally with salt and pepper before serving with a little butter.

Real Bread Pudding

Q. Do you know of a recipe for the real, stodgy, dark-brown bread pudding? The pudding I talk of usually has a sugar-encrusted top and is about 1½in thick. I have heard it called 'The Queen of Sheba's Wedding Cake'.

A. Soak 225g (8oz) bread crumbs in 250ml (8fl oz) milk for 30 minutes. Mix in 50g (2oz) brown sugar, 50g (2oz) raisins, 50g (2oz) currants, 50g (2oz) chopped suet, 1tsp mixed spice, ½tsp cinnamon and ½tsp nutmeg. Then mix in a beaten egg until the mixture is of a dropping consistency. Bake in a buttered 900ml (1½ pint) baking dish for an hour at Gas Mark 4.

Drinks

Bottle It

Q. I am keen to find a recipe for elderflower fizz and cordial as I have an excellent supply of flower heads. Can you recommend one?

LG, by e-mail

A. For elderflower fizz: grate the peel of two lemons, squeeze the juice and put both in a large sterilised bucket with 10 litres (18 pints) of water in it. Add 1kg (2¼lb) sugar, 5tbsp of white wine vinegar and five large, clean elderflower heads (to clean, gently shake each head). Stir gently then leave covered for 24 hours, stirring every six hours. Strain into sterilised glass screw-top bottles, or old sherry or port bottles with corks, making sure the corks are well pushed in. Store in a dark, cool but not cold place for six months.

For elderflower cordial: boil 1½ litres (2½ pints) of water and dissolve 2kg (4½lb) sugar in it. Add the grated lemon peel and two roughly chopped lemons to the hot water, followed by 100g (4oz) of citric acid and 20 large, clean flower heads. Cover the leaves to stand at room temperature for 24 hours, stirring occasionally. Carefully strain the cordial, ideally through muslin, and then bottle it.

Orange Brandy

Q. I wondered whether you can recommend a recipe using oranges and brandy.

LLB, by e-mail

A. This recipe from an estate in Scotland has been in circulation for many years and, like most good brews, needs time to mature.

Peel 14 oranges and 14 lemons as thinly as possible. Steep the peel in a large container with 14 bottles of brandy and 2.3kg (5lb) of sugar for about two months. Stir regularly to ensure the sugar has dissolved. Strain, bottle and keep in a dark place for two years.

As Clear as Mud

Q. I am trying to find the origin and meaning of the toast 'Here's mud in your eye'. I have been to a few parties where this toast has been used and many other guests were as ignorant of its meaning as I was. Can you enlighten?

DD, Highcliffe, Dorset

A. This drinking toast has a variety of meanings, but they all stem from the main source of expressing good spirit and humour and a way of wishing success or happiness to someone who is drinking with you. It has also been used in the world of horse-racing where the winning horse kicks mud in the eyes of the losing ones. It has been connected to farmers raising a glass to the success of a good harvest, with mud in the eye symbolising a plentiful crop.

This toast may have arisen from the story found in chapter nine of the Gospel of St John, where 'mud in the eye' is a medium of healing and well-being.

Need for Mead

Q. I have found some recipes for mead but they seem to vary enormously and are rather complicated. Have you a simple one?

HWN, Market Rasen, Lincolnshire

A. There are two main styles of mead, one which is fermented quickly and has the characteristics of beer and the other which is wine-like with a high alcohol content. Pure mead is made without any spices or fruit but there are many derivatives.

When making mead it is essential that all equipment has been well sterilised before use. Most recipes stress that the water should be un-chlorinated and recommend tap water that has been boiled and allowed to cool.

Add 1.8kg (4lb) clear honey to 4½ litres (8 pints) of water and stir until dissolved. Add 25g (1oz) hops, 13g (⅜ oz) root ginger and the sliced skin of two lemons. Boil for 45 minutes. Pour into a large jar, reserving some of the liquid. Allow to cool until tepid and add 25g (1oz) champagne yeast (the type of yeast makes a huge difference to final product). Leave in a warm room for between two and four weeks until the bubbling stops, topping up with the reserved liquid as required. Stir in 5g (⅛oz) of isinglass. Cork tightly and store in a cool place for six months, then filter carefully into bottles.

Equipment and ingredients can be purchased from the Hop Shop, tel 01752 660382, www.hopshopuk.com.

Drink Problem

Q. The lack of fruit last autumn was disastrous for making sloe gin and damson gin. I am interested to know what alternatives there might be to make now to ensure that I will still have something unusual and alcoholic in my cupboards.

GGD, by e-mail

A. Elderberries, blackberries, raspberries, bullace plum and Mirabella plum are all good fruits to combine with gin when in season, while lemon vodka and ginger vodka can be made any time of the year. For the lemon vodka thinly peel a lemon and drop the peel in a bottle of vodka. After a few days the vodka will have turned yellow, then taste daily until the flavour is right. This will take at least five days. Then strain into a clean bottle and drink ice cold from the freezer.

For ginger vodka, peel a large piece of fresh root ginger and discard the skin. Continue peeling the ginger until you have a pile of shavings. Place them in a large bottle, cover with 2.25 litres (half a gallon) of vodka and seal it. Shake the bottle once a day vigorously for two weeks. Strain and discard the ginger shavings.

Prepare a syrup by warming a good half cup of water and dissolving a cup of sugar in it. Allow this to cool and then add the syrup to the vodka to taste. The vodka can be drunk immediately or left to age for up to six months.

Raspberry Liqueur

Q. I would like to make a liqueur or cordial with raspberries. Can you recommend a recipe?

RJM, Tiverton, Devon

A. Raspberry liqueur can be served as a luxurious end to a dinner party or had as a treat in a hip-flask. It is straightforward to prepare. Use an equal volume of raspberries and vodka. Combine in a large jar or bowl, leave covered for about a week, then strain out the fruit. Dilute this liquid with an equal quantity of water and add 450g (1lb) sugar per 5 litres (9 pints) of liquid. Stir well, bottle and keep for two months before use.

Another recipe is of Russian origin. Half fill a 5 litre (1 gallon) bucket with the fruit of your choice and fill to the top with granulated sugar. Cover and leave for six weeks to ferment. Strain through a sieve, pressing out the juice, then re-strain the juice through a jelly bag to clear it.

Add the alcohol: vodka, rum or brandy, in a minimum of one part alcohol to three parts fruit juice. Bottle.

Alcoholic Raspberries

Q. I always end up with a surfeit of raspberries from the garden and wondered if you could suggest a recipe to make them into a liqueur?

PK, Margate

A. Try the following ratafia. Take 450g (1lb) raspberries, 570ml (1 pint) of brandy, 110g (4oz) sugar and six almonds. Put the raspberries into a bowl and sprinkle over the sugar. Press with a spatula until the juice begins to run, add the almonds and brandy and stir gently. Put the resulting mixture into a large jar and seal. Shake daily for about 10 days and leave for two to three weeks. Strain through a fine filter and, now ready to drink, store in a corked bottle away from the light.

Orange Gin

Q. On a shoot recently I was given a snifter of orange gin, a great change from sloe gin. I would like to have a go making this. Have you got a recipe?

LM, Barnstaple, Devon

A. Patience is the main ingredient required when making orange gin as it is best left to mature for at least a few years. For this reason it is also a good idea to make a large quantity.

I have been recommended a recipe which uses: 20 Seville oranges, 4½ litres (8 pints) gin, 1.35kg (3¼lb) granulated sugar and six cloves. Firstly, thinly slice the peel from the oranges, making sure no pith is attached. Place the peel in a demijohn, add the gin, sugar and cloves and cork the demijohn (this can be done using some kitchen roll wrapped in cling film). Store this in a cool dark place and shake regularly.

After about three to four months the sugar should have dissolved. Taste and then siphon off into bottles and seal. You might need to filter the gin through coffee paper to remove any sediment.

To ensure the gin keeps for years you can seal the top of the bottle with sealing wax, and add the family crest for an impressive finish. Orange gin really does improve with the years, so if you can wait you will reap the benefits. The peeled oranges can be used for making marmalade.

Rowan Vodka

Q. Last year I made rowan jelly but had copious numbers of berries left over. This year I would like to try making something else using the berries. Can one make rowan vodka and, if so, do you have a recipe?

FF, Holt, Norfolk

A. Rowan berries are very astringent. Before ripening they contain tartaric acid; after ripening they have citric and malic acids, the sugar sorbin and the saccharine principle sorbitol.

Ideally the berries are picked when fully ripe and after the first frost, but quite often if you wait until then the birds get there first. Therefore pick the berries when fully ripe but before the first frost. Rinse them carefully, remove the stems and put them in the freezer for a couple of weeks. The frost makes the berries milder and sweeter.

Put 800ml (approx 1¼ pints) berries in a glass jar with a tight-fitting lid. Cover the berries with vodka and allow to steep for one to four weeks in the dark at room temperature. Shake lightly and taste it occasionally. Strain and filter your infusion into a glass bottle. Store for a minimum of two months in a dark place at room temperature. Continue to store the vodka in this way, even during use, as heat and direct sunlight can cause unwanted change to its colour and aroma.

Beech-Leaf Booze

Q. I am interested to find a recipe for a liqueur using beech leaves. Can you help?

JPE, Huntingdon, Cambs

A. Young beech leaves can be used to make a liqueur called Noyau, which dates back to the 18th century. It is potent and, some say, similar to Japanese sake.

Pack a glass jar with young beech leaves which have been well washed. Fill it up with gin, cover and leave for two weeks. Strain off the gin and use coffee filter paper to strain and remove any leafy parts. For every 570ml (1 pint) of gin allow 225g (9oz) sugar dissolved in 285ml (½ pint) of boiling water.

Mix well. Add 1 tbsp brandy per bottle and cork tightly.

Ginger Up Cordial

Q. I make quantities of elderflower cordial but am trying to find a recipe for ginger cordial. I have searched many recipe books but none mentions a ginger one. Can you help?

JD, Crediton, Devon

A. I have two recipes for you, one I use regularly and another that has been recommended, both very different in their making.

For the first recipe you require one lime, 80g (3oz) caster sugar and a large piece of ginger, peeled and sliced crossways. In a saucepan place the peeled zest of the lime, the juice, sugar and ginger together with ½ litre (15 fl oz) of water. Stir over a low heat until the sugar is dissolved, bring to the boil. Then reduce the heat and simmer for 10 minutes. Remove from the heat and allow to cool. Strain into a sterilised bottle and store in the fridge. This ginger cordial can be frozen but may lose some of its strength.

The second recipe is for a ginger and lime cordial and makes about 200ml (6fl oz). You need 150ml (5 fl oz) of fresh lime juice (six to eight limes), 110g (4¼oz) caster sugar and a large piece of fresh ginger, peeled and roughly chopped. Whizz the juice, sugar and ginger in a blender until smooth and the sugar has dissolved. Pour through a fine sieve into a bowl and press firmly with the back of a spoon to gather liquid from the pulp. Discard the pulp and pour the cordial into a clean bottle. This should keep for at least a week in the fridge.

Both cordials mix well with sparkling water and also with dry ginger ale and soda water.

Blackberry Whisky

Q. I made some blackberry whisky in several years ago and felt disappointed that I had wasted some good whisky and blackberries. However, I had a bottle left which I used at our shoot in January of this year and a guest said it was the best he had tasted. Unfortunately, I have lost the recipe. Can you help find a replacement one?

MA, Faringdon, Oxfordshire

A. As with many concoctions, flavour develops and improves with age and blackberry whisky is definitely one that does. It is worth keeping for up to two years to be really appreciated, as you have found.

In a large screw-top jar mix one bottle of whisky, 225g (8oz) sugar and 1.8kg (4lb) blackberries. Shake every few days until the sugar has dissolved. Leave in a dark cupboard for three months and turn to mix every couple of weeks. Strain and bottle. It can be drunk immediately but patience really pays off.

Port Etiquette

Q. If the port fails to be passed around the table after dinner the expression 'Bishop of Norwich' is used to encourage the offender to pass it on. Can you tell me who was this Bishop of Norwich and how his name became linked to drinking port?

BVW, Chaford, Devon

A. Passing the port is one of the many British eccentricities of etiquette. The correct way is: the decanter of port is placed in front of the host who serves the guest to his right and then passes the decanter to the guest on his left who in turn pours out the host's glass, and so on.

One explanation for this is that it is seen as a sign of friendship and peace to the person on his left. Pouring with your right hand would prevent you being able to draw your sword or revolver. Also the majority of people are right-handed and find it easier to pour with the right and pass on with the left. It is considered bad form to ask for the port so the host asks the offender whether he knows the Bishop of Norwich. If the response is no the host responds, 'The Bishop is an awfully good fellow but he never passes the port.' The bishop in question was known for being stingy but no one seems to know which bishop. The current Bishop of Norwich has heard the story but his office is unable to shed light on it.

Some port enthusiasts say it can be the Bishop of Norwich or any other town as many bishops were known for being frugal. They also say that the link with port might relate to a time when port became popular in England after the Methuen Treaty of 1703 when merchants were permitted to import it at a low duty while war with France deprived the English of French wine.

Rum punch

Q. Please can you suggest some recipes for a good rum punch?

MG-B, Northam, Devon

A. Here are three to choose from, two cold and one hot:

Traditional: One of sour: one measure of freshly squeezed lime juice; two of sweet: two measures of syrup or sugar; three of strong: three measures of rum (Trinidad or Barbados); and four of weak: four measures of water. Before serving, add a dash of angostura bitters, a sprinkle of freshly grated nutmeg and a red cherry if desired.

Zombie: 20g (¾oz) each lime and pineapple juice, 50g (2oz) Puerto Rican rum, 25g (1oz) Jamaican rum, 10g (¼oz) apricot liqueur and some cracked ice. Serve unstrained with mint and a slice of orange.

Hot: Grate the rind of a large lemon into a saucepan and add 50 or 75g (2 or 3oz) of sugar, a pinch of ground cinnamon, a pinch of grated nutmeg, several cloves, 285ml (½ pint) rum, 285ml (½ pint) brandy, and 570ml (1 pint) of boiling water. Heat very gently and do not allow to boil. Strain the juice of a lemon into a punch-bowl, pour in the hot liquid and serve at once.

The following appeared in *The Field* in November 1952

RUM PUNCH

Cold Rum Punch: Pour one wineglassful of rum and one dessertspoon full of lemon juice over a heaped table-spoon full of crushed or shaved ice in a glass, add 1tsp caster sugar and shake well until sufficiently cooled. Strain into a small glass, float a thin slice of orange and a thin slice of pineapple on the top and serve.

Hot Rum Punch: Remove the rind from a large lemon by rubbing it with 50g (2oz) to 75g (3oz) loaf sugar, letting the sugar fall into a saucepan, add a pinch of ground cinnamon, a pinch of grated nutmeg, a pinch of cloves, 285ml (½ pint) of rum, 285ml (½ pint) brandy and 570ml (1 pint) boiling water. Heat gently by the side of a fire but do not let it boil. Strain the juice of lemon into a punch bowl, pour in the hot liquid and serve at once.

Sloe Gin

Q. I read recently that one can use sloe gin instead of cassis in a Kir Royale. Can you tell me the ratio of sloe gin to wine and give a recipe for 80 people?

JLD, Atherstone, Warwickshire

A. The original idea of Kir, named after Felix Kir, Mayor of Dijon, was to add cassis for sweetness to an inexpensive white grape of Burgundy. There are a number of variations on this theme. The most popular is Kir Royale (made with sparkling wine) and Kir Imperial (made with champagne and raspberry liqueur instead of cassis).

I have spoken to a London wine merchant and a well-known mixologist who have never come across this mixture and both feel it could be unpleasant. They recommended a sloe gin fizz, which consists of one part sloe gin, one part gin, ¾ part fresh lemon juice, one part syrup and three or four parts soda water. Or plump for the traditional Kir Royale. For 80 people you would need 12 to 18 bottles of fizz (ideally a decent cava) two bottles of cassis and, for a classic twist, add a raspberry to each glass to finish.

Reader's top tips

SLOES

Rather than throw sloes away after making sloe gin, put them in the freezer and then use them to add decoration or alcoholic content to cocktails. A well made sloe gin is irresistible and will soften the heart of even the most reluctant lady.

Nicholas Bray, Dorset

Sloe Gin Recipe

Q. I recall seeing a sloe gin recipe in a past issue but am unable to find it. Could you assist please?

IM, by e-mail

A. We have featured many recipes for liqueurs and hip flask tipples but never sloe gin. However, a member of staff regularly uses the following method: freeze the sloes so that they split and then put into a demi-john, filling it to about two thirds full. Cover with about 175g (6oz) white caster sugar and top up to the brim with gin. Shake well and leave to soak for a minimum of three months. Then remove the sloes, sample, and add more sugar to taste.

The sloes can be substituted with mulberries which make a delicious brew that we think is even better.

Lemonade Cooler

Q. I would like to make my own lemonade. Please can you advise me of a method?

SP, Greenford, Middx

A. Put the peel of three lemons without pith (if waxed, wash well and dry first) into a jug with 65g (2½oz) sugar. Cover with boiling water, stir to dissolve the sugar and then allow to cool. Add the juice of the lemons and cold water to taste. Strain, chill and serve with ice.

Alternatively make some lemonade syrup to keep in the fridge. Put the peel of five lemons into a large bowl with 700g (1½lb) sugar. Pour over 570ml (1 pint) of boiling water and stir until the sugar has dissolved. Add the juice from the five lemons and 25g (1oz) tartaric acid to the syrup and leave to cool, then strain and bottle. Use 1½ to 2 tbsp of syrup to make a glass of lemonade and top up with soda or carbonated mineral water.

Bullshot

Q. I am trying to find a recipe for Bull Shott; do you know of one?

JA, Exmoor

A. This originated in America and is usually spelt 'bullshot', so called because its main ingredient is beef consommé. Prue Coats in her book *Prue's New Country Kitchen* gives this recipe: mix 1 carton tomato juice with a tin of beef consommé and heat gently but do not boil. Add a squeeze of lemon juice, ½tsp oregano, ½tsp celery salt and a dash of Worcestershire sauce. Lastly add a generous slosh of vodka or sherry to taste. Serve warm.

Hair of the Lamb?

Q. Have you ever heard of a drink called Lamb's Wool which I understand is like mulled wine but made with beer? If so, do you know the recipe?

PBA, Farnham

A. Rosamond Richardson, in *Country Wisdom*, gives the following recipe: preheat the oven to 180°C/350°F/Gas Mark 4. Peel and slice two apples, put on a metal tray and bake for 30 minutes. Gently warm 570ml (1 pint) of beer and add ½tsp ground nutmeg, 1tsp ground ginger and 100g (4oz) brown sugar in a large saucepan. Stir until dissolved – about three to four minutes – being careful not to overheat. Float the apples on top and it is ready to serve. If you prefer, use cider and add a little ground cinnamon.

This punch, dating from the Middle Ages, probably gets its name from the floating pieces of apple which, after roasting, are puffy and very white – just like tufts of lamb's wool.

Chilli Sherry

Q. Do you have a recipe for chilli sherry and how much I should add to soup to enliven it on a cold day shooting or at the races?

GJD, Worcestershire

A. Fill a wine bottle with fresh chillies and top up with sherry. Cork securely and leave for about two weeks. This will keep indefinitely and more sherry can be added from time to time. For best results add just a few drops to soups, sauces and curries.

A less expensive alternative would be chilli vinegar. Add 25g (1oz) dried chillies to 570ml (1 pint) of boiling vinegar, allow to cool and then bottle. Leave for five to six weeks. Use only a few drops for seasoning.

A word of warning: as chillies contain oils that can irritate the skin and eyes, care must be taken when handling them.

Atholl Brose

Q. I have tried a number of different recipes for Atholl Brose over the years, but wonder if you can possibly tell me the definitive one?

MP, Dorset

A. The Duke of Atholl's recipe which is very filling is as follows: 275ml (½pint) whisky, 275ml (½pint) oatmeal, 1tbsp honey and 1tbsp cream.

First soak the oatmeal overnight in cold water and then put through a fine strainer. Mix the honey and whisky together thoroughly and add the strained oatmeal and cream. Omit the cream if you intend to keep this for any length of time as it is inclined to go sour and is only really added to give some colour.

Shake well before drinking and add a little more whisky if it has stood for a couple of days. It is best to use raw whisky as mild whisky does not work so well.

Groggy Old Seamen

Q. Is there any special reason why the Navy drank grog and why it is so called?

HN, Yorkshire

A. A gallon of beer a day was the original ration, necessary because the water, as a rule, was undrinkable. At sea, however, it was almost impossible to keep beer from going off and as Lord Howard wrote to the Admiralty in 1588 'nothing doth displease the seamen so as sour beer'. But it was not until the 17th century that wine was issued for ships going to the Mediterranean and then ½pint of neat rum morning and evening became the standard daily ration and was often doubled if the weather was unusually severe.

In 1740 Admiral Edward Vernon prohibited the serving of 'neaters' and ordered it to be diluted with water before issue. It came to be known as 'grog' after the Admiral's nickname of 'Old Grog' owing to his habit of wearing a Grogram cloak (made from a coarse material of silk and mohair). Grog tubs were wooden barrels with a band round the middle which read 'The King God Bless Him'. The ship's company would assemble around the tub and drink the health of the Sovereign.

Warming Tipples

Q. Can you suggest a change from mulled wine as a winter warmer?

EMA, Tasmania

A. 'Bishop' and 'Ginger Snap' are good alternatives. To make Bishop take three oranges, 24 cloves, ½ bottle inexpensive port, 1tbsp clear honey, 2 tbsp brandy, warmed. Stick the cloves into two of the oranges and bake in a dish in the oven at 350°F/180°C/Gas Mark 4, for about 15 minutes.

Heat the port and honey in a pan and add one of the cooked oranges, simmering for about 15 minutes. Put the second orange into a ladle and pour the brandy over it. Set the orange alight and, still burning, lower it into the port. Add a slice of the uncooked orange to each glass, putting the rest in the punch. Serves 12.

For Ginger Snap take 300ml (½ pint) water, 275ml (9fl oz) ginger wine, 2tbsp lime juice, 1tbsp brown sugar, and a pinch of nutmeg. Bring the water to the boil and pour over the other ingredients in a jug. Stir until the sugar dissolves. Serve hot.

....Reader's top tips....

TEA

To make tea with a difference, place sloes from gin in a tea strainer and pour your tea through it (no milk, no sugar). It makes a pleasant change from lemon.

Toddy Hoare, Holton, Oxford

Pass the Mint

Q. With the ever-increasing price of Pimm's and the decreased alcohol content, can you please provide a recipe that will enable me to make something similar?

RS-D, Berkshire

A. Recipes for home-made versions can vary somewhat. I suggest the following as a good alternative. Mix three parts gin (vodka if preferred) with three parts red vermouth and one part orange Curaçao; add a dash of Angostura Bitters and dilute with lemonade to taste adding ice. Garnish with fresh mint, slices of oranges and cucumber.

Reader's top tips

PIMMS

Pep up your Pimm's with a good slug of dry cider – it provides a refreshing bite to counteract the sweetness.

C Brides, Hertfordshire

Hangover Cures

Q. Can you recommend any hangover cures that really work?

CK, Gloucestershire

A. The after-effects of heavy drinking are caused not only by alcohol but also by preservatives and chemical by-products from fermentation, called congeners. Alcohol is a diuretic causing dehydration, while congeners taken in large quantities poison brain cells.

Brandy, blended whisky and red wines have high alcohol and congener contents and so tend to produce the worse hangovers. Gin, vodka, white wine and malt whisky, with fewer congeners, are less likely to cause bad hangovers. But these are only general rules, however, as the amount of congeners can vary from brand to brand, and their effect varies from person to person.

Never drink on an empty stomach. Drink as much water as you can before going to bed, and take a couple of Paracetamol if you have a headache, rather than Aspirin, which will irritate an already unsettled stomach.

Stimulants, such as caffeine in coffee, will not speed the rate at which alcohol is removed from the bloodstream, nor will a 'hair of the dog' alcoholic drink the morning after.

Jams and Preserves

Lady Marmalade

Q. I make vats of marmalade for my family and friends. I am fed up with chopping peel and there doesn't appear to be a modern peel shredder on the market. Can you help me find an alternative, easy recipe that doesn't involve all this hard work?

AWT, by e-mail

A. For a tasty, non-shredding marmalade cut 100g (3½ oz) dried apricots into medium sized pieces and put them in a bowl with 750ml (1¼pints) boiling water and allow to soak for about an hour. Pour 850g (1¾lb) canned prepared Seville oranges and 2.25kg (5lb) granulated sugar into a large preserving pan. Add the apricots and water and heat, gently stirring until the sugar has completely dissolved. Increase the heat and boil for 10 minutes, then remove from the heat and test for a set. Allow to cool, then pot and seal. This makes approximately 3.6kg (8lb) of marmalade.

Rose Petal Jam

Q. I have an abundance of highly scented rose petals in my garden and would like to use them in cooking. I believe one can make jam with them. Do you have a recipe?

LB, The Slaughters, Glos

A. To make rose petal jam collect 450g (1lb) of highly scented rose petals. Boil 600ml (1pint) of water in a pan. Take off the heat and add half the rose petals. Cover and leave to stand for two hours. Strain the liquid into a clean pan, discarding the steeped rose petals. Add 450g (1lb) of caster sugar to the rose-water and stir over a low heat until dissolved. Pour in the juice of two limes and the remaining rose petals, reserving a handful for later. Bring to the boil, reduce the heat and simmer until setting point is reached. Mix in the remaining handful of petals and simmer gently for another three minutes. Allow to cool for a few minutes before pouring into sterilised jars and sealing. The rose petals should rise to the top, leaving a clear jelly underneath.

Making use of Rose-Hips

Q. I have a large quantity of rose-hips in the freezer and am unsure what to do with them. I have been told that they make rather nice marmalade but have never seen a recipe for this. Would you know of one?

CB, by e-mail

A. This recipe, based on a Danish one, is like a cross between a jam and a conserve. It does not make a very solid set, but is full of fruit. It is ideally kept and eaten in late winter. Place 900g (2lb) of rose-hip shells, cleaned of all seeds, in a large pan with half a vanilla pod, 200ml (6fl oz) distilled malt vinegar and 285ml (10fl oz) water. Simmer until almost soft, then add 450g (1lb) preserving sugar. Continue cooking until the hips are very soft and the marmalade has thickened a little. Add the juice of 1½ lemons to taste.

Remove the vanilla pod and pot into porcelain jars if possible. Natural light can affect the colour, so if you use glass jars, store them in a dark cupboard.

In a Pickle over Chutney

Q. I can't find a recipe for uncooked sweet chutney (I am not keen on the smell of boiling vinegar tainting the house for weeks, even if the result is worth it). We are regular picnickers and love to have a jar of homemade chutney in our hamper. Can you help?

RMM, Langton Matravers, Dorset

A. This recipe requires no cooking or boiling. Mince 450g (1lb) dates, 450g (1lb) cooking apples (peeled and cored weight) and 450g (1lb) onions. Place in a bowl with 450g (1lb) brown sugar and 450g (1lb) sultanas. Add 425ml (¾ pint) of vinegar, one teaspoon each of ground ginger and salt and some freshly ground pepper. Stir well. Leave for 24 hours, stirring occasionally. Pot up into sterilised jars and leave for one to two weeks. Eat within two months.

Uses for Rosemary

Q. I have a large rosemary bush in my garden. It's a pleasure to look at when in flower and I use sprigs when cooking lamb. What other uses are there for it?

MH, St Ives, Cambridge

A. Rosemary is good for colds, fatigue, indigestion and as an anti-depressant when made into tea (put a teaspoon of leaves into a cup, add hot water and allow to infuse for 15 to 20 minutes). It improves circulation and can be used in facial steams; use two handfuls with six cups of boiling water and place in a bowl. With a towel over it, hold your head 12in from the water, close your eyes and relax for 15 minutes.

Rosemary oil is used in cooking and it is easy to make your own. Pick it, wipe it with a damp cloth and put in a warm, shaded place for several hours to allow the moisture to evaporate. Place eight sprigs of fresh rosemary (twigs removed) in a 600ml (1 pint) bottle with two scored cloves of garlic, a teaspoon of coarse salt and two teaspoons of black peppercorns. Cover with a fruity olive oil and seal. Keep in a cool, dark place for a couple of months before using. If you want to use it immediately, shred the leaves before adding them to the bottle.

To use in a marinade, pound two handfuls with a rolling-pin, mix with seven crushed garlic cloves, 250ml (8fl oz) olive oil, three lemons (halved, squeezed and the skins squashed) and freshly ground pepper. Rub on to the meat and leave until ready to cook.

Rosemary works well when added to stew and risotto and also in a vase with other flowers.

Raspberry Vinegar

Q. Could you supply me with a recipe for raspberry vinegar? It was readily available many years ago and was enjoyed on pancakes, drunk as a cordial and even used as an antiseptic. Nobody seems to remember these recipe gems from yesteryear. Can you help?

MDP, Louth, Lincolnshire

A. Fruit vinegars are simple to make. Pour 1 litre (1¾pints) white wine vinegar over 1 litre (1¾pints) raspberries which have been gently bruised with the back of a spoon. Allow to stand for four days, stirring daily. Strain through a jelly bag, adding 450g (1lb) of caster sugar per litre of liquid. Heat gently till just simmering. Allow to cool, then bottle and cork tightly. Store in a cool, dry place. Drink diluted with water. It is also effective for soothing sore throats, either taken neat or with a little hot water.

Lime and Lemon Marmalade

Q. Do you have a recipe for lime and lemon marmalade?

EY, Hutton Wandesley, York

A. This is a truly refreshing marmalade and can be made at any time of the year. The citrus fruit should be only just ripe and used as soon as possible. For the marmalade you will need 6 lemons, 6 limes, 1½ litres (3 pints) water, 1.35kg (3lb) granulated sugar and 5 half-litre jars.

Peel the fruit, then halve and squeeze out the juice and reserve the pips. Slice the peel thinly and drop the slices into a bowl of water as soon as they are cut to prevent them drying out. Chop the fruit pulp and tie in a muslin bag with the pips. Place the muslin, peel, juice and water in a pan and simmer for between one and two hours, until the peel is completely soft. Remove the muslin bag, squeezing hard to extract all the jelly-like substance and stir it into the pan. Add the granulated sugar, ideally gently warmed for 10 to 15 minutes. Stir until dissolved. Bring to the boil and boil hard for 10 minutes. Test for a set. Repeat at 10 minute intervals of hard boiling until a set is achieved. Leave to stand for a few minutes, stir, pot and cover. Label when cold.

Mulberry Recipes

Q. I have harvested a large quantity of mulberries from a tree in my garden and I would be grateful if you could suggest a recipe to use them up.

DP, Cambridge

A. I have found an old recipe for mulberry marmalade that seems quite easy. Stalk 1.2 litres (2 pints) of not over-ripe mulberries and chop them up. Stand them in a preserving pan at the side of the fire until sufficient juice for cooking has been drawn, and then simmer them until they are tender. Add 450g (1lb) honey and stir until blended. Then boil fast until the marmalade sets on being tested. Since honey is about one-fifth water, it is important that no extra water be added.

Meddling with Jam

Q. We moved house not long ago and have found a medlar tree in our new garden. We haven't had one of these before and wonder if you could tell us when the best time to pick the fruit is and what we might do with it?

JN, West Sussex

A. Pick the fruit in mid November. Put it on to clean silver sand 'eye' side down with the stems pointing upwards and place somewhere cool. When it has softened and lost its green tint it is ready to eat or cook.

If you have a good crop then jam is quick and easy. To 1.8kg (4lb) of ripe fruit add 1.65 litres (2¾ pints) water and the juice of six lemons. Add the chopped peel of three lemons in a muslin bag. Bring to the boil and simmer until soft. Remove from the pan and rub through a sieve to get rid of the skins and seeds. Return to the pan, first noting the weight of the pulp. Gradually add 350g (¾lb) granulated sugar for each pound of pulp, stirring well until dissolved. Bring to the boil and boil rapidly for around 10 to 15 minutes until the setting point is reached. Bottle and seal.

Medlar Jelly

Q. Our medlar tree produces a good crop and I'd like to make jelly or chutney. Have you a recipe?

PP, Malton, North Yorkshire

A. I cannot find anything for chutney but the following jelly recipe is from *Sensational Preserves* by Hilaire Walden. Medlars ripen in late autumn but remain hard, green, astringent and inedible. However, they brown and soften if bletted (stored in sawdust or straw for one to two months). If possible, use two-thirds bletted medlars and one-third firm fruit.

Ingredients: 900g (2lb) medlars (chopped but not peeled or cored) and sugar (warmed on the lowest heat of the oven for about 20 minutes). Put the medlars in a pan and pour in enough water just to cover them. Bring to the boil, cover and simmer for 30 to 45 minutes, stirring occasionally, until the fruit is soft. Tip the contents of the pan into a scalded jelly bag suspended over a non-metallic bowl and leave to strain in a cool place for eight to 12 hours.

Measure the juice and pour it into a saucepan. Add 450g (1lb) warmed sugar per 570ml (1 pint) and stir over a low heat until the sugar has dissolved. Raise the heat and boil hard for 10 to 15 minutes, stirring occasionally, until setting point is reached. Remove from the heat and skim off any scum. Ladle the jelly into warm, clean, dry jars. Cover and seal. Leave overnight to set. Store in a cool, dark, dry place.

Potent Ketchup

Q. I believe elderberries are used in Pontack Ketchup but cannot find a recipe; do you have one?

VG, Shalford, Surrey

A. The only – very old – recipe I know of is as follows. Put ripe elderberries, picked from their stalks, into a stone crock or several large jars and cover with best quality malt vinegar. Cover the crock or set lids on to the jars and put into a slow to moderate oven for two to three hours to extract all the juice. Strain while hot and measure into a saucepan. For every 1.2 litre (2 pints) of liquor add a teaspoon of whole cloves, 1 blade of mace, 1 tablespoon peppercorns, 1 dessertspoon allspice and 8 shallots, and boil until the liquor is well flavoured. Strain through muslin, measure and return to the pan; for every 1.2 litre (2 pints) of liquor in the pan add 225g (8oz) filleted anchovies and simmer until dissolved. Take off the heat and bottle at once; seal or cork tightly. Allow to mature for a month or two before using.

Avoiding Jelly Wobbles

Q. When I make jam or jelly, how can I tell whether the fruit has enough pectin in it to set well?

AL, Scarborough, Yorkshire

A. Here's a simple way to tell whether you have enough pectin. When you have simmered the fruit so it has broken down completely, squeeze about a teaspoon of juice from the fruit into a cup. When it is cool, add three teaspoons of methylated spirits, shake the cup gently and leave for one minute. If you have plenty of pectin, your mixture should look like a transparent jelly-like lump; two or three not very firm lumps indicate a moderate amount of pectin; if there are lots of small pieces there is insufficient pectin. To increase the pectin, simmer a little longer and test again.

As strawberries, raspberries and cherries are fairly low in pectin, it is a good idea to mix them with high-pectin fruit such as apples, redcurrants or gooseberries. You could also add some pectin stock made from cooking, windfall or crab apples or gooseberries. Simmer the fruit until pulpy and then strain through a jelly sieve. Bring the juice to the boil but do not add any sugar. Pour into warmed jars and seal. The pectin should be stirred in after the rapid boil stage of the recipe. Allow roughly a 275ml (½pint) sized jam jar of stock per 1.5kg (4lb) of fruit. Alternatively, use ready-made apple pectin extract called Certo.

Elderberry Jam

Q. I often see recipes for jam using elderflowers but do you have one which uses the berries?

RTT, Dunstable, Beds

A. Strip ripe elderberries from their stalks and weigh them. Put them into a large pan and then crush. For every 1.8kg (4lb) of fruit add the pith of three lemons and six tablespoons of lemon juice. Simmer gently and allow the fruit to cook until the skins are soft – about 10 to 15 minutes.

Sieve out the seeds and then add 1.46kg (3¼lb) of warmed preserving sugar to 1.8kg (4lb) of fruit and stir in quickly until dissolved. Bring to the boil and cook until a set is reached (seven to 10 minutes). Test by tipping a teaspoonful of jam. When it runs off in a sheet or flakes, it is ready. Fill heated jars to 3mm (⅛in) from the top and seal. Store when cold.

An Orange Alternative

Q. This is a wonderful time of year for oranges. I always make some marmalade but do you know any other sort of preserve I might try?

MF, Altrincham, Cheshire

A. The following recipe makes 1.3kg (3lb) of good, strong chutney – excellent with cheese or cold duck.

Peel 675g (1½lb) thin-skinned oranges using a zester and chop the zest finely. Peel the oranges again to get rid of as much pith as possible and then chop them into small pieces, saving any juice. Put the chopped orange, zest and juice into a large pan with 350g (12oz) cored, peeled and chopped Bramley apples and 350g (12oz) peeled and chopped onions. Cook gently until the onions are soft.

Stir in 225g (8oz) sultanas, 225g (8oz) dark soft brown sugar, 425ml (15fl oz) white wine vinegar, 2.5ml (½ level tsp) salt, 5m (1 level tsp) mixed ground spice, 2.5ml (½ level tsp) ground ginger and a generous grating of nutmeg. Continue stirring until all the sugar has dissolved and then simmer for about an hour or until there is no free liquid. Put into warm, clean jars, cover with vinegar-proof lids and leave to cool before putting into the store cupboard.

This recipe comes from *The WI Book of Salsas and Unusual Preserves* by Grace Mulligan of *Farmhouse Kitchen* fame.

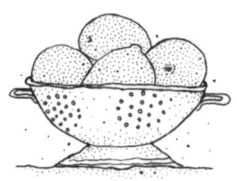

A Game Alternative

Q. At this time of year I always have to cook all manner of game. I am tired of the usual accompanying blackberry and blackcurrant sauces and wonder if you can offer a recipe for something different.

SH-M, Berwickshire

A. Apple and juniper jelly makes an interesting alternative. Chop 900g (2lb) Bramley apples and put them into a pan with 570ml (1 pint) water. Add a muslin bag containing 75g (3oz) crushed juniper berries. Simmer until the apples are soft and then strain.

Measure the resulting juice and pour into a clean pan, adding 450g (1lb) of preserving sugar for each 570ml (1 pint). Bring quickly to the boil and continue boiling until it reaches setting point. Take off the heat and stir in 2 tbsp of gin and 2 or 3 drops of juniper oil. Bottle and seal.

Tomatoes Out to Dry

Q. Sun-dried tomatoes are very popular at the moment but terribly expensive. I grow Gardener's Delight tomatoes which are very tasty and wonder if it is possible to use up the surplus by drying the tomatoes myself?

TM, Hampshire

A. Cut the tomatoes in half and scoop out the seeds, leaving as much flesh as possible behind. Sprinkle sparingly with salt and place them face down on to wire racks to drain.

Transfer the racks into an oven pre-heated to its lowest temperature. Prop open the oven door slightly and let the tomatoes dry out for six hours. When they feel dry but still slightly fleshy, remove and cool. Put into jars and cover with olive oil. Add some basil and garlic if required, and shake gently to remove any air bubbles. Cover and seal before storing in a dark, cool place for a month before using.

Ketchup with a Kick

Q. I have a good supply of walnuts and have heard it is possible to make a walnut ketchup. Do you have a recipe for it?

PDB, Peterborough

A. Choose and crush about 70 green walnuts, picked in about mid-July. Add 175g (6oz) salt, 175g (6oz) chopped onion, a peeled clove of garlic and 1¾ litres (3 pints) of spiced vinegar just brought to the boil. Stir well and when the salt has dissolved, allow to stand for a fortnight, stirring thoroughly each day. Then pour off the liquid into a pan and simmer for an hour. Bottle and seal.

Essence of Mushrooms

Q. I have a collection of old recipes for soups, some of which use mushroom essence, but I cannot find a recipe for it anywhere. Do you know of one?

CCB, Norfolk

A. Try the following recipe: 1.8kg (4lb) field mushrooms, 110g (4oz) sea salt, a litre (1¾ pints) red wine vinegar, 2tsp of a mixture of equal quantities of ground ginger, mace, allspice and black pepper, three cloves of garlic and 2tbsp port.

Slice the mushrooms thinly and place on a large platter, cover with salt and leave for six to eight hours; then rinse. Put the mushrooms together with the vinegar, spices and garlic into a large saucepan, cover and simmer for about an hour to an hour and a quarter, stirring frequently. Leave to cool, strain and add the port. Store in fairly small corked bottles and seal with wax. Once opened keep in the fridge.

Mushroom essence is also a very good addition to casseroles and stews.

Mushrooms to Savour

Q. We live in an area where there is a good supply of field mushrooms every autumn. Can you advise a good way of preserving them?

JEG, East Sussex

A. Thread them on to fine string using a darning needle, leaving space between each one so that they do not touch each other. Hang them in a dry current of air until they are completely shrivelled and then push them together like a string of beads. Hang the string on a hook inside a wrapping of black tissue paper to keep out the dust. Be sure to soak in wine, stock, milk or water before using.

Tangy Mint Sauce

Q. I had gooseberry mint sauce in a restaurant recently and wonder if you have a recipe for this delicious accompaniment to roast lamb?

GM, West Midlands

A. Put 450g (1lb) of gooseberries in a pan, cover them with water and simmer until soft. Strain the fruit and measure the juice, adding 450g (1lb) of sugar to each 570ml (1 pint). To this add the juice of a lemon and a small bundle of mint. Cook gently to dissolve the sugar, then boil until it sets. Remove the bundle of mint, finely chop the leaves from six fresh stalks of mint and mix them into the jelly. Then pot for future use.

In a Pickle

Q. I wonder whether you can find me a modern recipe for pickled walnuts? I have access to a plentiful supply of growing nuts, but over the past two years the resulting pickle has been quite uneatable because I have followed Mrs Beeton's advice.

TRW, Hampshire

A. Pick the walnuts when green, before the shells begin to form and become woody.

Freely prick them all over with a long carpet or packing needle. Place in a large jar and cover with brine, made from 175g (6oz) plain cooking salt to each 1.2 litres (2 pints) of water; leave for six days, then drain. Cover with a fresh solution of brine and leave for six to seven days. Drain again and set the nuts on large plates or plastic trays, and place in warm sunshine, turning occasionally to give them exposure.

When black and dry, pack in pickle jars and cover with spiced vinegar. To make the vinegar, place 25g (1oz) allspice, 25g (1oz) peppercorns and 20g (¾oz) crushed root ginger to each 1¼ litres (2 pints) of vinegar, in a loose bag of muslin, bring to the boil, boil for about 10 minutes. Allow to cool, remove the spices, and use the liquid to cover the walnuts, and cover the jars. Leave for at least six weeks (it improves with keeping). Wear plastic or rubber gloves when handling nuts as walnut juice is very staining.

Decorative Mint

Q. Can you tell me how to prepare and preserve mint leaves for garnishing party puddings?

AW, London

A. Lay the leaves in a shallow baking tin. Brush with unbeaten raw egg-white and sprinkle thickly with granulated sugar.

Dry out completely in the oven at 240°F/110°C/Gas Mark ¼. The leaves are best stored in an airtight tin until required.

Damson Cheese

Q. My mother used to make damson cheese for a Christmas treat. I would like to try making this for my grandchildren, but I can't find a recipe.

TJA, Penbridge, Herefordshire

A. Fruit cheeses need to be cooked slowly and watched over carefully. Defrost 2kg (4lb) damsons and place in a saucepan with 300ml (½ pint) of water. Heat to simmering point and cook gently until soft, mashing occasionally. Rub through a sieve and weigh the pulp. For every 450g (1lb) pulp you need 350g (12oz) sugar. Place the pulp in a clean saucepan and cook gently, stirring until thick. Pour in the warmed sugar and stir well to dissolve. Turn the heat up a little, and stir until the spoon leaves a defined mark when pressed down on the mixture. Spoon into a shallow mould that has been lightly wiped with groundnut oil. Seal the cheese using wax paper (wax side down). Cover with cling film. If you can wait, leave it to allow the flavour to develop.

Ginger up Marmalade

Q. Do you have a recipe for ginger marmalade using root ginger?

GC, Portsoy, Banff

A. Squeeze 700g (1½lb) of Seville oranges and put the juice into a pre-serving pan (reserving the peel, pips and any pulp), along with the juice of one large lemon and 1.7 litres (3 pints) of water.

Finely slice the orange peel and add to the pan with 150g (5oz) of peeled, shredded fresh ginger. Put the pips and pulp into a muslin bag and attach it to the pan handle so it dangles in the liquid. Bring to the boil and simmer for one to one and a half hours until the peel is soft and the liquid has reduced by half.

Remove from the heat and squeeze the juice out of the muslin bag into the pan. Return the pan to a low heat and add 1.35kg (3lb) sugar, stirring continuously until dissolved. Continue to stir while boiling hard for 12 to 15 minutes until setting point is reached. Test by putting a spoonful of the mixture on to a chilled saucer and prod to see whether the surface wrinkles. Take it off the heat and skim to remove any scum. Let it stand for 15 minutes, then give it a final stir. Spoon into warm, dry jars. Cover and seal.

Guava Fruit Cheese

Q. I love the flavour of guava. Can you suggest a way to use it other than making jam?

LS, Portsmouth

A. Guava is generally used for jams and jellies but a fruit cheese would make a refreshing change.

Cut up 1.8kg (4lb) of guava and put in a pan with one level teaspoon of citric or tartaric acid, or four tablespoons of lemon juice. Just cover the fruit with water. Simmer gently until the fruit is soft and has broken down into a pulp. Pass this through a fine sieve.

Weigh the mixture and for every 450g (1lb), add 450g (1lb) of sugar. Put back into the pan and stir over a low heat until the sugar has dissolved. Then, stirring continuously, boil the mixture until it reaches a semi-solid consistency. Add a pinch of cinnamon or ground ginger. Spoon the cheese into jars and seal while still hot. For a more buttery consistency reduce the quantity of sugar and boil only until the required set is reached.

Gardening

Blind Daffs

Q. I have had several clumps of blind daffodils this year. Please can you tell me the best time of year to fertilise them for flowering in future years and what type of feed I should use. I usually mow my daffodils at the end of June.

FI, Dumfriesshire

A. Blind daffodils occur for a variety of reasons: cutting their leaves rather than letting them die down, congested clumps or a dry summer. This results in the bulbs not having enough energy to produce flowers. March is an ideal time to feed the bulbs with a granular high-potash feed and then liquid feed with Miracle-Gro or Phostrogen every couple of weeks until the foliage dies down. Ideally the foliage should not be removed for at least eight weeks after the bulbs have finished flowering. The bulbs could also have become overcrowded so it might be worth lifting the affected clumps in the autumn, dividing them and replanting farther apart. It is worth watering if the summer is dry as this helps the bulb take up nutrients in preparation for flower production.

Moss Loss

Q. I have an 18th-century cobbled path in my garden. The majority of the stone is set in soil and there is no easy way of weeding short of using weedkiller, which I don't want to do. Can you suggest a way to prevent winter moss from growing on it?

TS, by e-mail

A. The moss does not damage the path but can make it slippery. Most methods for removing the moss and weeds from a cobbled path involve exercise and determination. A hard block-paving brush with a long handle, narrow head and wire bristles is effective for clearing off moss without stooping, though some of it might need to be loosened with a sharp knife first. A pressure washer is an effective way to remove moss, but in areas where drainage is unsatisfactory use it carefully, as the extra water could increase damp problems. You could apply pelargonic acid, an organic acid found in Weedol MAX, to the area. It will kill the moss and some weeds. For tougher perennial weeds buy a ready pack of glyphosate and spot treat them.

Apparently soda crystals can work well in removing and preventing the build-up of moss. Soda crystals are free of bleach, enzymes and phosphates and when sprinkled on to moss, then left for a few days, will turn the moss brown. This can either be scraped off with a shovel or brushed off. The crystals should keep the area clean for at least a year, though it is advisable to spot treat a small area first to check nothing unwanted happens.

Mole Control

Q. Can you suggest a ploy that might keep moles off my garden, or tell me a way of dealing with them?

JB, Barton-on-Sea, Hampshire

A. Try the following method (which has had mixed results): deter moles by mixing 100ml (3 fl oz) castor oil and 8 litres (14 pints) water and drenching each molehill with it. It won't kill or hurt the moles but it might encourage them to dig elsewhere.

Dog Damage

Q. While a friend was house-sitting for me over the summer, her dog decided to sabotage part of my small garden – it dug up bulbs, chewed and discarded them and overturned and emptied various pots in the process. She was apologetic, but neither my friend nor I is much of a gardener. Can you give me some pointers as to when I should buy the replacement bulbs and how to plant them for a spring or early-summer display, as this is when I am at home to appreciate them.

CC, by e-mail

A. Spring-flowering bulbs need to be planted in the autumn, tulips should be planted in November, and summer-flowering bulbs in early spring. When purchased, most bulbs are in a dormant, leafless and rootless state and should be planted as soon as possible. They are ideally planted in groups at approximately two or three times the height of the bulb deep, and twice the height of the bulb apart from each other as a rough guide.

Label the bulbs when planting so you remember what they are. If they are planted in a border it ensures that you don't dig them up after flowering. In pots or in situ, these bulbs are ideal: winter aconite, cyclamen, snowdrop, iris, snakeshead fritillary, muscari (grape hyacinth), crocus, anemone, lily of the valley, ranunculus and dwarf tulips look wonderful in pots but they need very good drainage so use soil-based compost with a generous helping of grit.

Reader's top tips

TOMATO JUICE

A splash of tomato juice in a dog's daily feed prevents the dreaded 'pee circle' on manicured lawns.

David Leslie, Aydon, Northumberland

Potted Produce

Q. I am keen to grow vegetables next year but haven't the time to spend preparing an area of ground to plant them in. I assume they can be grown in pots and I have a porch and sheltered yard that would seem ideal.

ZP, by e-mail

A. Pots, troughs and growing bags can be used to grow fresh vegetables. Containers need to be of a certain size – ideally a depth and width of 50cm (20in) – otherwise frequent watering and feeding will be needed. Use sterile potting compost for good results, soil-based John Innes No 3 works well.

Crops that grow well in containers are: beetroot (sow in March with 10cm (4in) spacing); peas (sow cultivars with edible pods from March, 15cm (6in) apart); spinach (sow from mid-February, 5cm (2in) apart); potatoes (one tuber for every 30cm (12in) of pot-diameter using an early cultivator – they can be planted from March); runner beans; broad beans (can be sown from February, 15 to 20cm (6 to 8in)apart). Herbs are ideally grown in containers from March onwards and many are ready to pick from June.

All seeds should be kept well watered, but not waterlogged. If frosts are likely, ensure the plants are covered at night or make sure they are placed in a sheltered spot. Feed with a liquid fertiliser every two weeks.

Using pots is a versatile and successful way of growing edible produce, especially if space is restricted.

Hedge Doctoring

Q. We have a large hedge with a great deal of hawthorn in it, which has slowly got rather out of control. A part of it has been damaged recently and we want to replant that section. We would appreciate some simple advice on how to maintain the existing hedge before it starts to upset the neighbours.

WL, by e-mail

A. Hedge plants such as hawthorn flower and fruit on the previous year's growth and the cutting of these should be undertaken in late winter after the berries have been eaten. Care should be taken to avoid pruning during the nesting season between March and August. It is very tempting to prune a hedge so it has a square top but in fact a flat-topped 'A' is the most suitable; the sides of the hedge should taper in towards the top, allowing light and rainwater to reach lower foliage.

If the hedge is cut at the same height and width each year the growing tips can become woody and eventually will not produce new growth. Therefore, to encourage a bushier hedge, cut about 2.5 or 5cm (1 or 2in) above the previous year's growth. If there are gaps in the hedge you can generate new growth by cutting stems to within 15 to 20cm (6 to 8in) of the ground. This fresh growth will help create a thicker hedge. If there are young plants in the hedge, prune hard, then remove at least half of the new season's growth every winter to encourage lower branches.

When replanting a hedge make sure you remove half the height of the plant after planting. This will protect it from winter winds that can loosen the roots and make them susceptible to damage. Keep all young hedge plants moist and mulch well to prevent weeds.

Growing Hawthorn

Q. How difficult is it to grow a hawthorn hedge?

TD-C, Essex

A. Hawthorn (*Crataegus monogyna*) does not readily root from cuttings and is propagated from seeds. Gather the ripe haws or berries in early winter, place in layers in a container or box, covering each layer with damp sand, place in a cool spot for six months or more, then rub out the seeds, free of pulp.

Sow the seeds in rows on to a well-raked, weed-free seedbed, about 4cm (1½in) deep in a warm, sheltered corner, and leave to germinate and grow. Transplant the seedlings in October to March, 20 to 30cm (8 to 12in) apart, where they are to grow on. Hawthorn will grow in almost any situation. Wait until after June before trimming the young plants into shape.

Coffee Grounds

Q. As a coffee drinker I generate a lot of coffee grounds. I have been told they make a good fertiliser. What plants are they best used on?

WL, Otterburn, Northumberland

A. Coffee grounds are full of nutrients, particularly nitrogen, and are best used on acid-loving plants such as blueberries, roses, rhododendrons, azaleas and camellias. Coffee grounds can also be used to improve productivity when growing carrots – simply mix the seeds with the coffee grounds before sowing. They add nutrients to the soil as they decompose around the plants, and the coffee aroma can deter ants, other insects and even cats from using the garden. Coffee grounds have many other uses, such as reducing the dust when cleaning out a fire – sprinkle the wet grounds over the ashes before removing. Fresh or used grounds can also be used to absorb unpleasant smells from a fridge or freezer. To do this, place grounds in a bowl and leave overnight.

Sucking a coffee bean has similar effects to a peppermint for refreshing breath, while a small heap of coffee beans rubbed together in your hands can help neutralise strong smells such as fish and garlic.

Mint Source

Q. We have a basic variety of mint in our garden and want to add different varieties to create an area with a wonderful aroma of mint. What others are there and where can I buy them? And what is the best way to deal with rust on mint?

MF, Melton Mowbray, Leics

A. There are more than 50 different varieties of mint in the UK and some imports from USA, where a lot of breeding takes place – including Hilary Sweet Lemon, named after Hillary Clinton. Some of the more traditional mints are ginger, eau de cologne, black peppermint, pineapple, peppermint and spearmint. Also popular are apple, banana, basil, lavender, lime, orange and buddleia. Chocolate peppermint is a seller with its dark bronze leaves and its After Eight scent; Moroccan is ideal for making mint tea; and Corsican is a ground-hugger with small leaves and an extremely strong scent.

The Herb Nursery in Rutland supplies all of these mints and a large variety of wild ones. The majority of its plants are propagated and grown on site. Contact The Herb Nursery, Thistleton, Nr Oakham, Rutland LE15 7RE, tel 01572 767658. Mint can also be ordered online from The National Herb Centre's website, www.herbcentre.co.uk.

Mint with rust should be cut off at ground level and the old leaves cleared away. Feed with high-nitrogen fertiliser.

Going Bananas

Q. As an unusual Christmas gift I was given a banana plant, *Musa basjoo* and some seeds. I am slightly at a loss to know what to do with them. Are you able to help?

HRR, Cheltenham, Glos

A. *Musa basjoo*, a native of China, is a hardy banana and excellent for beginners. You can leave it out all winter but as new it must not be planted in the garden until after the last frosts.

This tall, slender banana with bright green leaves is a very architectural plant to have in the garden in a warm, sheltered position. It quickly develops suckers to form a clump effect similar to bananas in the tropics. You need to protect the main stem in winter with a wire-netting-style tube stapled to a tree stake, filled with straw and covered with plastic to keep the water out but allowing the plant to breathe. In May remove the wrapping. It should then grow to reach flowering size. Water regularly in dry weather, mulch well and feed with a high nitrogen liquid feed.

Normally the plant would be cut down after the first frost damage and the rootstock protected with straw or bracken during the winter. Shoots from the base have been known to exceed 1.8 or 2.1m (6 or 7ft) by September.

To germinate a banana seed gently file to make a small nick in the seed coat and soak in warm water for 24 hours. Sow in individual small pots of potting compost and germinate at a minimum temperature of 21°C. The plants will grow fast and soon need repotting into larger pots.

Rose from the Dead

Q. We have recently inherited a garden of untidy roses, some of which appear dead and need replanting and others that could do with a good prune. We would like to know the best time and way to do these two things. Are you able to help?

JD, Exmoor

A. January and February are good months to prune but if the weather is cold and frosty it is advisable to leave it until March. The rose bushes ideally need to be shortened by a third to two thirds, or three to four buds from the base, removing all the weak, old, woody and dead steams as well. Always prune with sharp secateurs and make cuts above a bud and on an angle away from it. Remember to dead-head the roses during the flowering season and remove any further dead or diseased branches if necessary. When replanting new roses in ground where others roses have previously been it is important to prepare the ground properly to prevent rose sickness. One way to do this is to change the soil to a depth and width of approximately 60cm (2ft) minimum, adding a good application of Rootgrow and a well-rotted manure or garden compost when you plant the rose.

Alternatively, dig a large hole and place a good-sized biodegradable cardboard box in it, one large enough not to disturb the root ball of the new rose, and then add healthy soil and compost. When you firm in the roses make sure the graft (the piece between the root and the stem), is slightly above soil level. New roses should be pruned hard when first planted – down to a third of the original height – to ensure they don't become leggy in later life.

Reader's top tips

ROSES

Plant garlic and chives around your roses to keep aphids and black spot at bay as well as improving perfume.

Alexandra Thrower, Salisbury

Sugaring Moths

Q. We want to attract more moths to our garden. Can we do this by putting in certain plants?

MH, Fowey, Cornwall

A. Plants that smell strongly at night are ideal for attracting moths to your garden. The tobacco plant *Nicotiana* is one of the best for moths and is particularly liked by the rare convolvulus hawk moth. Ivy and sallow blossom, sedum, night-scented stocks, honeysuckle, hebe and red valerian are also favourites of moths. Buddleia attracts moths and butterflies.

Another way of encouraging moths to your garden, particularly in late summer and autumn, is to paint trees, walls and gateposts at dusk with a sugary solution made by mixing stout, molasses and brown sugar together in a pan, simmering for about half an hour and finishing with a dash of rum. Exact quantities are not important, just ensure your mixture is not too runny. 'Sugaring' is most effective on a warm, cloudy, calm night. The solution can stain, so choose your sites carefully.

Pollarding Trees

Q. We have two trees that have rather outgrown their space and we have been advised by our neighbours to pollard them. Can you explain this practice and do you feel it would be the advisable thing to do?

GW, Cheltenham, Glos

A. Originally pollarding was a method used to protect valuable timber from damage caused by animals such as deer and rabbits and allowing space for grazing cattle beneath. For pollarding, the branches are severed from the trunk at about 2m (6ft 6in) high, which differs from coppicing where the branches are removed at ground level, The ideal time to undertake this task is late winter or early spring when food reserves are high and the tree has a plentiful supply of water. It is not recommended to pollard trees in the autumn as the wood is usually at its driest, allowing easier access for fungi that causes serious decay. Young trees respond rapidly to this process, thus reducing the risk of infection and onset of decay. It is important to continue the cycle of pruning otherwise, if left, the branches will develop a dense form, reducing light levels beneath. Branches should be cut above the previous pollarding wounds as this avoids exposing old wood, which is more susceptible to decay. Not all trees are suitable for pollarding and it would be wise to check first. Pollarding is easy to maintain and prevents trees from outgrowing their allotted space while allowing growth to the desired height and branch framework.

Deer Devastation

Q. My house sits in the middle of a farm surrounded by forestry. We love to see the wildlife in our garden but are unable to have flower beds as the muntjac and fallow deer come and help themselves. As we don't want to fence the garden are there plants we could have that the deer would not eat? If so, what are they?

ADSU, by e-mail

A. Deer have a preference for certain plants so planting unpalatable ones can help reduce deer damage. The range of unpalatable plants is restricted and will limit the diversity and appeal of the garden if they are the only choice. These plants include camellia, fuchsia, hellebore, hosta, hydrangea, iris, lavender, poppy and rhododendron. Another way to protect your flowers and maintain a diverse garden is to provide an alternative browse for the deer by allowing brambles, rosebay willowherb, rowan, dandelion, campion, knotweed, sweet lupir, redleg and yarrow to grow in the garden. The deer will prefer these and should avoid your favourite vulnerable plants.

This mixture of effective plant protection should help reduce deer depredation and provide an attractive boundary. An added benefit is that a more varied garden would be richer in insects and birds. With this extra safeguard other plants should flourish. A list can be found on The British Deer Society's website, www.bds.org.uk.

Watercress

Q. As a child I use to pick watercress from a steam near home. Now I have a stream running through my garden and wonder whether I can plant or sow seeds for my own crop. Can you help?

CCD, by e-mail

A. Watercress likes to grow in rich soil along stream-beds and in the sun. Seeds can be sewn directly into the wet soil near the stream about two weeks after the last frost. Sow them thickly, approximately 5mm (¼in) deep. As the watercress becomes established the plants will spread and float on the edge of the stream, rooting in to the soil below.

Watercress seeds can also be started indoors in peat pots or spread over very damp kitchen towel, which should remain wet at all times. Germination should take place in about ten days and these roots will then require transplanting into individual peat pots and growing on for about three weeks before planting outdoors. As the plants mature, trim the older ones back to about 10cm (4in) in height and they will leaf out again.

An ideal container in which to grow watercress is a small paddling pool with a couple of holes in the bottom to ensure that the water doesn't become stagnant. Fill with a suitable compost or soil and soak. If your greengrocer can supply you with watercress with a few roots then that is ideal. Plant them directly into the soil and keep them well watered.

If you sow seeds in early to mid May and lightly cover with soil, the watercress should be ready to harvest in July.

Holm to Moth Disease

Q. Our holm oak tree is looking rather miserable as the leaves are showing some damage. There are pale-brown, discoloured patches on the leaves and we have been told it could be a moth disease. Would this be correct and, if so, what can we do?

KJC, Sherborne, Dorset

A. If evergreen oaks have been affected by the leaf-mining moth the damage appears at its most extensive at this time of year. The leaves will have pale brown, elongated-oval areas, or 'mines' on the upper leaf surface. This is where the caterpillars have eaten the internal leaf tissue The tiny leaf-mining moth, whose forewings are 3mm (⅛in) long, has yellow central bars, purplish wing-tips and pale, feathery underwings. It has three generations a year; the larvae feed within the leaves during July, October and from late November to March. When they are fully fed they pupate within the leaf mines.

Unfortunately there are no insecticides available to home gardeners that are likely to control them. However, holm oaks tolerate the damage and continue to grow, even when heavily infested. Their appearance improves as new foliage develops.

Reader's top tips

INSECT DETERRENT

Insects dislike walnuts, so plant walnut trees in paddocks and other areas where livestock graze to provide the beasts with insect-free shade.

Bruce Wilkinson, Glapthorn, Northamptonshire

Ivy on Trees

Q. Ivy is strangling my trees. I have cut the shoots around their bases. Is there some chemical I can spray on the ground around them that will kill the ivy but not harm the trees?

EJM, Withybrook, Coventry

A. There is much debate as to whether ivy actually strangles trees. Ivy requires plenty of light to climb up a tree trunk, so is more commonly found in hedgerow trees where there is plenty of side light. It is also found on dying trees when the canopy is thinning out, allowing more light through.

Ivy is a very valuable habitat for wildlife as it is a late-flowering plant. Bees and other insects visit in autumn, while its berries are eaten by overwintering birds. Its intertwined stems and evergreen foliage make it an ideal place for nesting birds. Ivy is not a parasite; it takes nothing from the tree but uses it only for support. When ivy gets in to the canopy of a tree it can reduce the amount of light reaching the lower leaves and its weight can make an old tree more liable to be blown over in the wind or shed branches. This is indicative that the tree was old or unhealthy.

As ivy is shiny some chemicals stick better to the leaves than others. Both Roundup and Tumbleweed are ideal and can be used if the bark on your trees is healthy, reasonably thick, woody and not green at the bottom. The spray is taken up by the green parts of the plant and will not damage the tree. Ivy in the canopy can be pulled out but this is not essential.

Weeding out Ivy

Q. I am trying to kill some ivy which been growing for many years up a high wall with ornamental brickwork at the top. I would be grateful if you could advise me of the best make of weedkiller to use. When would be the best time of year to apply it?

MEF, Yorkshire

A. To kill ivy top-growth and roots, sever the main trunk or stems within inches of the ground or base. Drill the root stump with 9mm (⅜in) holes, slanting downwards to the woody core, about 5cm (2 in) apart around the stump and fill with the total weedkiller sodium chlorate. Seal with tape and leave the chemical to be absorbed by the cambium layer of the stem.

The top-growth can be killed by placing the cut main stems on the plant in a can or plastic container and leaving it to absorb the solution. When the foliage browns and dies, the ivy shoot can usually be detached with light pulling for collection and burning. The solution should not be allowed to wet and dry on clothing (or animal coats) as there is a slight fire risk.

Espalier Trees

Q. We have a collection of unruly espalier trees in our garden. Can you advise how and when they should be cared for?

DD, Brackley, Northants

A. Late summer is the ideal time to prune espalier trees as this prevents the upper tiers from being overproductive at the expense of the lower ones and encourages the development of fruit buds on short spurs. If you prune too early the leafy shoots may regrow and require more pruning later in the season.

Pruning should be done when the bottom third of each shoot has become woody but the tip is still flexible. Cut long shoots back to about three leaves from where they originate on the main stem or lateral. Any shoots that have arisen from short side shoots should be cut back to one leaf from where they originated on the main stem. Cut just above each leaf and in the same direction as it is pointing. Ideally don't prune shoots that are shorter than about 23cm (9in) long. If they grow sufficiently they can be cut back later in the season.

This pruning will make the espaliers look better and, if they are fruiting trees, will improve the harvest for the following year. If they are looking tired loosen the earth round the main trunk and mulch with a good compost, but don't put the compost too near to the trunk as this can cause damp and rot.

Composting

Q. We have recently moved to an area of the country that is hot on recycling and it feels as though most of my time is spent sorting rubbish. This has spurred me to think about composting and I wondered whether you have any suggestions that could get us going – we have five children so we seem to produce large quantities of waste.

TCB, by e-mail

A. Composting is a very rewarding and important way of recycling and can make a positive contribution to helping the environment. There is also the added bonus of reducing your household waste by about 30 or 40 per cent. You can compost a range of kitchen waste including fruit and vegetable peelings, egg shells, tea bags, coffee grains, scrunched-up paper, hedge trimmings, grass, leaves and clippings. The key to good compost is the right mix of ingredients as you need to create a good carbon (brown – dried flowers, woody stems and cardboard) to nitrogen (green – kitchen waste and grass cuttings) ratio.

Compost can be made in a compost bin or in a secure, covered clamp to keep out scavenging dogs. It works best to start with if you add lots of material at once. Large items need to be chopped small as this helps speed up the process. The compost should be kept moist, if possible from rotting fruit and vegetables, but if it looks too dry add water. Conversely if it looks too wet add more material.

To help speed up the compost add an accelerator such as young nettles or a handful of soil. Continue adding a good mix of materials. Compost is ready when it resembles dark soil. This can take anywhere between six and twenty-four months depending on the contents and the temperature. Do not add meat, bones, fish, dairy products, cooked food and cat and dog litter and excrement to your compost, partly because they attract rats.

Growing Garlic

Q. I am very keen to attempt to grow some garlic, preferably in a large terracotta pot, in my small but sun-drenched and sheltered garden. Can you suggest how I go about this?

DP, Burford, Oxfordshire

A. Garlic is a relatively easy plant to grow and enjoys a well-drained, fertile, sunny position. It needs to grow quickly to produce good-sized bulbs, in a position that is well drained. Any waterlogging will cause the bulbs to rot. Garlic can be planted in autumn or spring, though autumn planting often produces larger bulbs.

For spring planting in a container use normal potting compost and buy a large garlic bulb from your local greengrocer. Gently remove the outer skin from the bulb and then separate the individual cloves. Choose the eight largest cloves, which are normally on the outside of the bulb. Plant the cloves in an upright position 2cm (¾in) below the soil, with the top of the clove facing upwards. Space the cloves 10cm (4in) apart.

Feed the garlic once or twice a month with a general purpose fertiliser, keep it free of weeds, and water in dry conditions. Harvest it when most of the foliage has turned yellowy-brown, which is around late August. Loosen the surrounding soil with a trowel and ease the bulbs gently out of the ground.

You can use the garlic immediately or it can be washed, dried and placed in a warm, dry place. These bulbs should keep in good condition for a minimum of three months.

Worm Casts

Q. I have been looking for a preparation to rid my lawn of worm casts. These are very unsightly and I believe affect the drainage. Garden centres have been unable to help; can you suggest anything?

RTJ, Watford, Herts

A. Generally, earthworms are good for lawns as their burrowing helps with drainage, aeration and the incorporation of organic matter such as dead leaves. They ingest soil rich in organic matter. Dead vegetable material may be collected at night from the soil surface and later consumed.

Food is broken down in the gizzard; organic matter is digested and absorbed into the blood but indigestible material (mainly soil particles of mineral origin) is passed out. The species *Allolobophora* deposits this at the soil surface as worm casts. These can appear in gravel paths but are more often found on lawns and are most noticeable on fine turf. Casts are mainly found when the soil is warm and moist (September, March, April and May) and the worms are near the surface. At other times the worms go deeper and casts are much less apparent.

Mowing or walking over the casts when they are wet spreads them, making the area slippery and providing good conditions for moss and weeds. If they are dry you can break up and disperse them using a broom or rake.

Pesticides to deal with such nuisances are no longer available except via a professional contractor who holds a Certificate of Competence; if the problem is very serious using a contractor may be your only option.

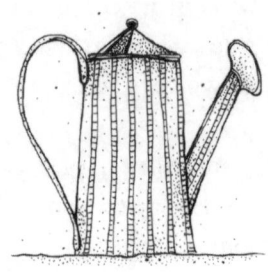

Roses at Christmas

Q. I have some Christmas roses which, although they flower, never give a good display. How can I encourage better flowering?

FS, Malmesbury, Wiltshire

A. The evergreen *Helleborus niger*, also known as the Christmas rose, is an excellent garden perennial as it is in bloom from late autumn to early spring when everything else is frozen solid. It can, however, be shy flowering and needs the right soil: deep, fertile, well draining and moist, neutral or slightly alkaline, enriched with leaf-mould or compost. It can be situated in partial shade or ideally under a deciduous tree so that it gets some sun but is protected from strong winter winds. Christmas roses have a deep-growing root system and are not keen on being disturbed so, while it is worth trying to transplant yours, it may not be successful and you might have to start again. Please note that the roots of this plant are poisonous.

Wait until early spring when the ground is not too hard to plant or transplant. For fresh, young plants, leave about 30 to 40cm (12 to 15in) between each one and point the roots downwards rather than spreading them out. Also make sure the crown is about 2½cm (1in) below the surface, then mulch. Each spring, remove the old foliage and feed with a soluble fertiliser.

If you are unable to provide the right soil and situation it may be better to plant Christmas roses in pots using a loam-based compost.

There is a legend attached to the Christmas rose about a young shepherdess named Madelon who was tending her sheep one cold and wintry night. As she watched over them, a group of wise men and other shepherds passed by, bearing gifts for the newly born Jesus. Madelon wept because she had nothing to give, not even a simple flower. An angel heard her weeping, and brushed away the snow to reveal a most beautiful white flower tipped with pink – the Christmas rose.

Field Mushrooms

Q. We have some pasture grazed by sheep and ponies. I'd like to encourage field mushrooms to grow on it. How do I do this? Is there a company that sells spores? Or would field mushrooms 'take' if I just got some ex-mushroom farm compost and spread it around?

CMB, Alresford, Hants

A. Ann Miller, a mycologist, says that mushroom compost would only produce cultivated mushrooms (*Agaricus hortensis*) although these are unlikely to become established, having been developed to grow in industrial mushroom farm units.

Field mushrooms (*Agaricus campestris*), whose spores are in the air, will grow on most types of soil (although clay can often be too wet or too dry) but only in a spot to their liking. However, much depends on the weather which is why a well-colonised field will produce a good crop in some years and nothing in others.

It is essential to provide the right conditions to encourage growth. Ann Miller suggests seeding some small patches of spawn around the field during spring or summer for autumn fruiting. Cut out sections of turf (about 25cm (10in) square and 4cm (1½in) deep), fork into the soil below some well-rotted horse or farmyard manure, add about 50g (2oz) mushroom spawn, and replace the turf, making sure to water during dry weather.

The spawn will develop on the manure and establish a fungal mat under the soil's surface. This will produce mushrooms when the weather triggers fruiting. If conditions are right the mat will spread and colonise where it finds other patches of 'food', and mushrooms will appear in fairy ring fashion around the field year after year.

It is impossible to say how long it would take to colonise a field completely as it depends on many factors including the weather, the soil type and nutrients and other fungi in the soil, but with luck you should be picking some soon. Do remember that wild mushrooms should be positively identified before being eaten.

Spawn and colonised logs for growing mushrooms such as shitake, tree oyster, lion's mane, shaggy inkcap, wood blewit and parasol, and seedling trees with roots colonised by truffles – no pigs required – are available from Ann Miller Speciality Mushrooms, Greenbank, Aberdeenshire AB1 5AA, tel 01467 671315.

The Unkindest Cut?

Q. I have an old mulberry tree which bears most of its fruit on just a few of its branches. Should I prune it or leave it alone?

PMM, Ely, Cambs

A. Old and well-established mulberry trees should not be pruned hard as they bleed excessively from cuts; the more cuts you make the more the tree will suffer.

However, after the leaves have fallen, cut out any weak, dead or diseased shoots. If you want to thin out any live shoots, it is best to do this before the sap begins to rise again (usually in mid-December). Remove the live shoots at their base and paint the cuts with tree tar or antiseptic. Do not prune heavily in any one year; instead spread it over several years. If the branches bearing the fruit become so heavy they are in danger of breaking, it is a good idea to support them with wooden props.

Bugged by Bunnies

Q. My garden is chain-link fenced but baby rabbits can get through the mesh. They remain for a week or so and are then too big to get out again. I cannot net or snare them and at 76 am too old to shoot them. Have you any bright ideas?

WG, Reading, Berkshire

A. Put pegs all round the section of the garden you want to keep rabbit free. Attach to the pegs, about 15cm (6in) above the ground, string that has been soaked in creosote. The string must be changed every three days so have a second piece of string soaking in creosote ready to replace it.

As rabbits hate the smell of creosote you shouldn't have to do this for too long. But you will have to repeat the process yearly when the baby rabbits appear.

A Beginner's Orchid

Q. I was given a moth orchid for Christmas and was told it could be kept in the drawing-room. How do I look after it?

CCB, Denmead, Hampshire

A. The moth orchid (*Phalaenopsis*) should thrive indoors if a few simple rules are followed.

Put 5cm (2in) of gravel or perlite in the bottom of a bowl and keep it wet to provide humidity. Sit the plant on top of a saucer to keep the roots away from the water and place in the bowl. Place the orchid in a warm room in light or shade but not in direct sunlight or a draught.

Give the plant half a cup of tepid water when the compost has almost dried out, adding Baby Bio at every other watering. Ensure you do not get water on the leaves or flowers and never stand it in water or spray it.

When the orchid flowers the blooms last for several weeks and then slowly die one by one. When you have two blooms left on the spike, cut the spike off just below where the first flower bloomed. This will cause a new set of buds to form which should flower within fourteen to sixteen weeks.

Butterfly Plants

Q. Sadly, we do not get many butteflies in our garden. As I would like to attract a greater variety, what should we plant to encourage them to come and stay?

RCG, Haslemere

A. Butterflies are on the wing from March to October and are attracted by plants which are high in nectar throughout this period. Select a sheltered, sunny area and plant: primroses, aubretia and sweet rocket for spring; for summer: buddleia, lavender, catmint, thyme, heliotrope and red valerian; and for autumn: hyssop, michaelmas daisies and sweet scabious.

Persuading your butterflies to stay and breed is more difficult. The female is particular about where she lays her eggs as different caterpillars like different plants to feed on. Plants such as hedge garlic, hedge mustard and lady's smock are good for green-veined white and orange tip butterflies. Meadow grass, cocks-foot, false brome and Yorkshire fog will encourage meadow, hedge and wall browns, marble whites and large and small skippers, while holly and ivy are good for the holly blue butterfly.

Thistles encourage painted ladies, and stinging nettles, if planted in an old tub to stop them spreading, are good for small tortoiseshells, peacocks and red admirals. In late June or early July cut down part of your nettle patch (removing any caterpillars first) so that the next generation of small tortoiseshells can benefit, as they prefer young nettle growth.

Giving Lots of Figs

Q. We have a fig tree in our garden which we believe to be about 100 years old. It is situated against a south-west facing wall and is now in a very straggly state having had no attention for many years. However for the past twelve years we have had a good crop and this year it was a bumper one. Can you advise about pruning and how to ensure such bounty in the future?

BAV-L, Newark

A. Figs are unusual in that they contain the potential for two crops per year. Unfortunately we only ever see one in the UK as we simply do not have enough sunshine. The tiny fruits you would have seen before Christmas were the second crop which were unable to mature. This summer's first crop are currently microscopic buds in the axils of the leaves at the tips of the shoots and these are very susceptible to frost. Generally, a good crop follows a winter of little frost.

It sounds as though your tree needs a fair amount of attention but if you prune it now you will sacrifice this year's crop. I suggest that you wait until the spring and if the crop looks fairly light, sacrifice this and prune quite heavily. When the new shoots appear train these back against the wall. Repeat this regime, though less severely, for a second and possibly a third year.

To protect a future crop from frost you could drape the new shoots with straw, bracken or horticultural fleece in winter until the frosts are over; you should then be able to harvest a good crop in August/September.

Missing Mistletoe

Q. We live in mistletoe country but neither I nor my gardening friends have been able to grow it. Have you any suggestions?

J G, Co Tipperary

A. Berries from cut mistletoe cannot be used to propagate this plant; they must be taken from healthy growing specimens only. Moreover, use berries which have been growing on the same species of tree as the one you intend to grow mistletoe on.

Well before Christmas, cover the berries with a muslin bag to protect them from the birds. Pick the berries at the end of March when they are really ripe. Press them into a crevice on the underside of a mature branch at least 10cm (4in) in diameter and 1.5 or 1.8m (5 or 6ft) above the ground.

Make sure the skin breaks and the juice and seeds are rubbed in well. Perhaps tie some moss over this spot for protection. As little will be seen for about 12 months, it is a good idea to mark the branch with a dab of paint. If the mistletoe takes, a swelling will appear under the bark and some green shoots will emerge the following March or April. If it is still growing in May and the branch is getting thicker, the host tree has accepted the mistletoe. But be warned, it is very slow growing.

Mistletoe is a parasite and, as such, will feed on the branch, which will eventually weaken and struggle to survive. Once the mistletoe is well established, cut it frequently to help prolong the life of the branch.

A Much Loved Rose

Q. I have a favourite rose bush in my garden. Rather than buying another I would like to have a go at propagating it myself. Can you tell me how to go about it?

AK, West Sussex

A. Choose a sheltered, shaded bed and dig to a depth of 45cm (18in) adding one part builders' sand to each of soil.

Cut a perfect stem of not less than 30cm (12in) that has at least five leaf-clusters on it and put it into water immediately for an hour or so. Then snip off at an angle just above the topmost bud and just below the bottom leaf cluster. Strip off all but the topmost leaves and dust the bottom with hormone rooting powder.

Plant this in your prepared soil to just below the second leaf scar from the top. Press down the surrounding soil and water well. Put a large pre-serving jar over the top, lifting each day to wipe away any condensation on the inside.

When a second new leaf appears this means that the cutting has rooted successfully and you should remove the jar. Leave undisturbed for nine to twelve months before transplanting to another spot.

Reader's top tips

PLANTS

When potting plants put used tea bags in the bottom of your pots. They help to keep the compost moist and eventually break down and mix in.

Kay Grant, Hay-on-Wye, Hereford

Frozen Flowers

Q. Last winter I lost a number of perennials in the garden to frost, as I am limited as to how many I can bring indoors. Can you suggest other ways of protecting them?

MM, Devon

A. A small amount of light fabric over the crowns of any slightly delicate perennials is a good idea and packing straw or bracken among the leaves or branches would also help. Plants such as fuchsias will benefit from simply delaying pruning until the spring and putting peat around the base of small shrubs will make all the difference.

Probably the most important factor is where you site your plants. Damage to the plant tissue is more often caused by rapid thawing than by extreme cold. A quick thaw does more damage than a slow one, so you should avoid putting delicate plants in the lowest-lying areas of the garden where cold air collects, or where the early morning sun will thaw them out too quickly.

A Glut of Gladioli

Q. Gladioli seem to have an annoying habit of coming out all at once. Is there any way of delaying some of them?

DH, Chesterfield

A. The only solution I can suggest is to pick some of them when the buds are just showing some colour and leave them somewhere cool and dark for up to a week. All that is necessary to revive them is a long drink of warm water.

To make them last as long as possible cut their stems under water and re-cut every three or four days. Nipping out the top bud and removing the lower blooms as they wilt helps the gladioli to open.

Blistered Holly

Q. I am somewhat baffled regarding some leaves appearing on my holly trees with what looks like a light green blister. Can you offer me some advice?

DM, Ramsbottom

A. This is almost certainly caused by one of the many species of sawflies (*Tenthredinidae*) which resemble flying ants. They insert their eggs into the plant tissue and the resulting caterpillars feed on the leaves. Most species feed on the leaf surfaces and can be controlled by spraying with Malathion but there are some species, as in your case, which feed inside a gall (if you scrape the 'blister' away you will find the insects underneath). These can only be controlled by a systemic insecticide such as Bio Long Last which is available at most garden centres.

Rotten Onions

Q. How can I prevent my home-grown onions from rotting at the neck while tied up in storage?

AM, North Yorkshire

A. The problem is not the storing but is actually due to onion neck rot. The causal fungus only becomes evident once the onions are in storage although it actually begins on the onion seed and continues to grow slowly in the tissues of the plant while it is still in the ground.

To eliminate the fungus you should dust the seed before planting with green or yellow sulphur (obtainable from garden centres). To protect onion sets soak them in a suspension of the same fungicide before planting. It is also a good idea to get rid of any remains from last year's crop by burying or composting.

Fairy Fungus

Q. A fairy ring has appeared on my lawn which I presume is caused by *Marasmius*. Can you suggest a method of eradicating it?

AR, Bucks

A. The fungus responsible is indeed *Marasmius oreades*. The ring of mushrooms is the outward sign of a fungal infestation below the ground. When a fungal spore lands on suitable soil it starts to grow, radiating outwards as it develops. The fruiting bodies or mushrooms appear on the very edge of the fungal mass (mycelium) so forming a ring.

Even when the mushrooms die down the rings can easily be identified: the inner circle of grass will have died back, choked by the thickly woven mycelial mass, while the area of grass just outside the ring will appear exceptionally green.

Fungicides are not very helpful as they need to penetrate deep into the soil to reach the main mass of fungi. One (laborious) way is to dig the fungus out. If you have several rings it may be wise to re-turf the lawn. However, there is nothing to stop a stray spore landing in your garden in the future.

Dutch Elm Relapse

Q. Dutch elm disease is on the rampage again. Nearly twenty years ago I clear-felled a five-acre strip of dead and dying elms and replanted with a mixture of hardwoods in which dozens of healthy-looking young elms have naturally regenerated. A few now have trunk diameters in excess of 30cm (12in). So far, I have only had three infected trees this year and I have felled these.

Is it inevitable that all elms will eventually become infected with the disease, or is there anything one can do to protect one's trees?

LLS, Wiltshire

A. Dutch elm disease, caused by the fungus *Ophiostoma novo-ulmi*, claimed the majority of English elms in southern England in the Seventies. The surviving root systems produced suckers which have now grown to sizeable trees. Since these young elms are identical, genetically, to their parent trees they are vulnerable to reinfection.

The surviving fungus in the stump and existing root system can break out, killing the new shoots and suckers, although as the old infections become buried more deeply in new healthy wood the risk lessens.

The fungus can also be reintroduced by elm bark beetles (*Scolyrus* spp) through the transport of logs with infested bark. An infected tree can also spread the disease through a common root system to other trees.

Unless there is a change in the pathogenic ability of the fungus it seems likely that English elms will remain at risk.

When Daffodils Die

Q. What is the correct way to look after daffodils when they have finished flowering?

AW, Dorset

A. Dead-heading or cutting off the faded flower heads as soon as you notice them, but retaining the leaves and stalks while still green ensures that the plant continues to manufacture food by photosynthesis which goes into the bulb forming for next year and improves its quality. Do not remove leaves as they begin to yellow and wither. They can be loosely bunched and tied with raffia or twine until they die down and can then be removed.

Poor flowering performance is often caused by overcrowding in a naturalised planting. Lift the clumps, sort the bulbs to size and replace only the best. The smaller bulbs can be replanted but may take two or more years to build up to flowering well.

Any More Cyclamen?

Q. I am told that the popular winter-flowering indoor cyclamen can be kept to flower year after year. How is this achieved?

NM, Cambridgeshire

A. *Cyclamen persicum* and its varieties flower increasingly year by year if, when the spent flowers are removed, the plants are given regular watering and an occasional feed of liquid fertiliser. The plant likes a cool room and a north-facing windowsill is an ideal position. A warm room means a short life for a cyclamen.

When the leaves begin to die back, water less and put the plants in pots outdoors, sunk to the rims of their pots in a sheltered, sunny border in May. In late July or August, re-pot in fresh balanced compost with the tops of the corms at soil level.

Water on a weekly basis and grow on, keeping the plants weed free, then move to a shady greenhouse or a cool, sunny room in September, where the plants can be kept for the winter.

Mysterious Lawn

Q. I have a biggish lawn of mostly moss surrounded by beech woods. Recently, I looked out of my window one morning to see the lawn covered in neat, round tufts of grass, but no sign of digging. When I went out to investigate, I counted 101 tufts of grass scattered all over the lawn. When I looked closely, I found a slit in the lawn near each one, about 5cm (2in) long and fairly deep.

None of my friends have ever seen anything like it. Their guesses are squirrels, woodpeckers and crows, but I cannot think that it is an animal as there is no evidence of digging. Can you suggest what it might be?

HG, Oxfordshire

A. It is possible that the trouble with your lawn is caused by chafer grubs, of which the most likely is the cock chafer or maybug. This is often sought in grass land and lawns by such birds as thrushes and blackbirds. The insect lays eggs in early summer to hatch in four to six weeks and live in larval form for one to five years, feeding on plant roots.

They move up and down the soil and have been known to pupate as deeply as 60cm (24in). They come nearer to the surface in the summer. They are not too easy to control, but the application of an appropriate soil insecticide in early summer, when the bugs are first seen, may be helpful.

Another possible culprit could be leather-jackets – the larvae of crane flies, but these are generally found nearer the surface and are more easily seen.

Fertile Holly Berries

Q. I have holly trees on my land, probably self-sown, which are healthy and growing well, but failing to berry. Why is this so, and what can I do to remedy the situation?

MH, Wiltshire

A. A likely cause is that the trees only bear male flowers. The native holly (*Ilex aquifolium*) is usually unisexual. Check at flowering time in spring. Male flowers have four white stamens, spreading like a cross. Female ones have green ovaries at the base with four carpels (seed-bearing structures).

Some are hermaphrodite with both male and female organs. Only these and female flowers produce berries. Replacing male trees with female trees or grafting shoots from a female on to a male tree would improve cross-fertilisation, but it is a tricky operation.

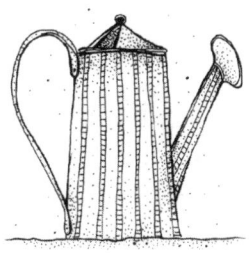

Seasonal Shrubs

Q. Can you give me a list of shrubs likely to flower at Christmas?

HBA, Rutland

A. The witch-hazel, *Hamamelis mollis* and vars *pallida*, and 'Moonlight', with yellow spidery flowers, rarely fail. *Mahonia japonica*, yellow, well-scented, lasts a long time. *Viburnum x bodnantense*, upright, rose-tinted white, in forms 'Dawn' and 'Deben', *Chimonanthus praecox*, and var *grandiflorus*, is sweet-scented, and deserves a warm, sunny wall. Winter jasmine (*Jasminum nudiflorum*) with its bright yellow flowers, will grow tall trained on a sunny wall or frame.

Reader's top tips

GARDEN KNEELING PAD

Make a cheap, effective and disposable kneeling pad for the garden by putting several folded newspapers into a carrier bag. This is easy to carry around as well as being simple to dispose of.

Kay Grant, Hay-on-Wye, Hereford

Making Flowers Blue

Q. What can be done to ensure blue flowers on hydrangeas?

WH, S. Yorkshire

A. Hydrangeas tend to produce blue flowers naturally when grown in well-drained, acid soil, well supplied with humus-forming organic matter (rotted manure, compost or peat) but lacking in lime. The key nutrient is aluminium. This can be provided by raking in powdered aluminium sulphate in the dormant season or before planting. Some varieties blue better that others. Choose from 'Generale Vicomtesse de Vibraye' or lacecaps such as 'Blue Wave' or 'Lanarth White'. Conversely, adding lime to a soil increases the colour performance of pink-flowering varieties.

From the Archives

The following appeared in *The Field* in October 1953.

BONFIRES

Q. Please could you advise how to create a really good bonfire to get rid of rubbish and garden waste?

WL

A. Start with a freely burning fire. When you have a good core of burning wood and 'coals' you can put on a thin layer of brushwood and then carefully heap on any rubbish or garden waste that needs burning – anything which is green or damp or which will be slow in combustion, such as green wood, weed plants, diseased material – even sods, couch grass etc. – or if the soil is heavy and clayey, you can add this in thin slabs. The slow-burning material should be placed all over the central core of glowing coals to exclude air completely, being arranged in layers over the top and down the sides to maintain a mound of material. The fire needs stoking at sundown and in the morning, fresh material being placed wherever there are signs of a break-through. If the fire is not allowed to burn and blaze away, it can be kept going for weeks.

Slippery When Wet

Q. My stone steps, flagged patio and paths become greenish and slippery in wet weather. How can I prevent this?

EBH, Lancashire

A. Wet the surfaces with a solution of one part tar-oil wash to eight parts water, by volume, with a watering can or hose and leave to dry. This kills the algae, fungi and moss, which cause the discolouration. With an occasional repetition, further fouling will be prevented.

Cutting Back the Winter Jasmine

Q. How should I prune my winter-flowering jasmine (*Jasminum nudiflorum*)?

CBH, Merseyside

A. As soon as the flowers fade, the shoots bearing them should be cut to just above two buds of their base. This is in February or early March. Overgrown, tangled, older shoots may be cut hard back to above well-placed younger side-shoots, and the new growths trained in.

···· *Reader's top tips* ····

MANURE

Fill a stocking with manure and hang it in a water butt for a few weeks. Stir occasionally and you will have liquid manure on tap.

Mr G Woods, London

... *From the Archives* ....

The following appeared in *The Field* in November 1986.

GROWING AVOCADOS

Q. How can an avocado pear be grown from the stone?

TTF

A. Plant the stone, pointed end upwards, in a 12.5 or 15cm (5 or 6in) pot filled with a suitable compost or with a mixture of equal parts by volume, garden loam and moist peat, plus a third part of coarse sand to about 2.5cm (1in) below the surface. Then place in a room with a minimum temperature of 24°C (75°F) until a shoot appears, when it can be grown on at a temperature of about 21°C (70°F) in good light but not in direct hot sun. As an indoor plant, it can be grown only as a foliage plant with a minimum winter temperature at night of about 13°C (55°F). Water freely in warm weather months and much more moderately in winter. It will not flower or bear fruit unless it can be grown on for a few years under hothouse conditions.

Mop-Head Hydrangeas

Q. When and how can I prune mop-head hydrangeas?

ECD, Ireland

A. The garden varieties of *Hydrangea macrophylla* are best pruned in late March, when new growth is just starting. It is worth bearing in mind that the plants will flower from any terminal buds formed the previous year which are left intact.

The flowered shoots and spent flower-heads are removed, together with any damaged, thin, weak or ingrowing shoots. Well-established, mature bushes can be reduced in size by cutting some of the branches back to their base or just above a suitable lateral shoot, chosen to retain the symmetry of the bush.

Garden Gypsum

Q. I am told that gypsum would be beneficial for my garden, long nurtured by regular organic manuring. How and when should I use it?

MK, Surrey

A. Powdered gypsum (calcium sulphate) is a good alternative for lime especially on soils over-enriched through the years by organic manures and compost. It reduces the stickiness of heavy clay soils where sodium salts have accumulated from the over-use of fertilisers. The calcium ions replace those of sodium to make the soil more friable and workable.

Gypsum may be used for lime-hating plants which need calcium, such as azaleas, rhododendrons, heaths and heathers, especially on heavy clay or over-acid soil, applied at 150g per m² (4oz per yd²). Gypsum makes an excellent substitute for lime or chalk at 150–300g per m² (4–8oz per yd²), for vegetable crops, fruit bushes and trees and flower borders and ornamental shrubs and trees.

Apply about once every three years. It can be applied at any time of the year.

Animals and Natural History

Creepy Clusters

Q. As I child I adored ladybirds. The thought of squashing one or letting my mother vacuum them up was horrible. How things have changed. My house is inundated with a variety of different-coloured ones and they seem to appear at any time. Why is this and do they bite? I think they do.

JHS, Suffolk

A. In the autumn and winter, ladybirds can gather together in clusters in the house, particularly around windows, curtains and under and behind beds. When disturbed from their dormancy, usually by the central heating, the Harlequin ladybirds are hungry and can bite humans in their search for something to eat. The bites slightly sting and usually produce a small bump and there are some documented cases of people having a severe allergic reaction. The ladybirds also have a defence mechanism of exuding a yellow fluid which has an acrid smell. The Harlequin ladybirds disperse rapidly over long distances and have a longer reproductive period than most other species. This makes them a nuisance in the house and a threat to our native ladybirds.

Buzz Off, Hornets

Q. The past couple of summers have been ruined in the evenings by hornets. They seem drawn to the house when the lights are on or if we are entertaining in the garden. They might only sting when provoked but we have had to despatch more than 10 some evenings. How can we stop them?

WB, by e-mail

A. Hornets build their nests in the spring and die off by late autumn. Hornets like nesting in sheltered places such as tree trunks, bushes, sides of buildings, barns, attics and hollow walls. They live off insects and sap and are not attracted to human food. By early summer a typical nest will be 30cm (12in) across (they can be much larger), with a colony reaching a size of 700 workers.

If you have a large quantity of them in your garden it is likely that there is a nest nearby. It is not advisable to kill a hornet anywhere near its nest as it produces a pheromone when killed that can trigger the entire nest to attack. If the nest is putting people at risk then it should be destroyed. Locate the nest by watching the flight path of the returning hornets. It is preferable to destroy a nest earlier in the year before the hornets become aggressive. Rentokil Pest Control offers services for DIY or professional treatment. Call 0800 218 2210.

Loss of Great Tits

Q. I have a cedarwood nesting-box that was used last year by great tits. They returned again this year and hatched their family and I enjoyed a few days of watching their comings and goings. Then the weather changed – it was rainy and cold for a couple of days before warming up again. Instead of seeing the tits resume their activities I found the nesting-box being frequented by numerous hornets. Eventually I took it down and discovered the whole tit family – adults and chicks – dead. Could the hornets have been the cause of this?

RB, Tiverton, Devon

A. Great tits are very susceptible to changes in the weather, particularly in May when they have young chicks. The RSPB says it regularly hears reports of families of great tits found dead at that time of year.

The birds' major food supply while they are nesting is caterpillars. If the rain has been heavy the caterpillars tend to be washed off the leaves, leaving the great tits wet and hungry. The RSPB recommends leaving out live mealworms for the birds, particularly when they have young, to compensate for any dramatic changes in the weather. It has never heard of any deaths of great tits by hornets and says that, though it is possible, it is highly unlikely. Hornets tend to attack only when aggravated and they might have been drawn to the nesting-box as a possible home as their nests have regularly been found in them. It would be highly unlikely for hornets to sting the birds.

The RSPB says that great tit numbers fluctuate each year and the weather is normally the culprit for any mass deaths.

Damsels and Dragons

Q. Last summer our garden was inundated with either dragonflies or damselflies. We are unsure why this was, but are hoping for a repeat performance this year. Is there an obvious difference between the two?

MSR, Saxham, Suffolk

A. Although the dragonfly and damselfly belong to the same insect order, Odonata, they are two separate insects with definite differences. The dragonfly has unequal wings. The hindwings are shorter and broader than the forewings, and at rest the wings are held out at right angles to the body. Most dragonflies have large eyes which touch. They are strong flyers and can be found well away from water, whereas the damselfly, being a weak flyer, prefers to stay close to the water's edge. Damselflies have four neat, paired wings and their eyes don't touch. At rest their wings lie along their body.

The majority of a dragonfly's life is spent underwater, firstly as an egg, then as a larva where it moves and feeds on live prey, before emerging from the water and shedding its skin to become an adult. Some dragonflies are known to swarm and this is normally due to good feeding conditions in the area.

For further information and to partake in an online species survey visit the British Dragonfly Society's website, www.dragonflysoc.org.uk.

Antler Points

Q. Some years ago we had a very enjoyable day, following the Devon and Somerset Staghounds. Some of the red deer were magnificent, with impressive antlers. How are the antlers counted, when are they cast and what makes good ones?

DLJ, by e-mail

A. Antlers, commonly known as horns in the West Country, are cast when testosterone levels fall – in the middle of March through to April –

with the older stags casting first. A new velvet-covered replacement starts to grow almost immediately. Velvet is a sensitive, soft, blood-filled, bone-forming tissue. Once the horns have grown to full size, by about July, the blood supply stops and the stag sheds the velvet by rubbing it against trees. This does not occur until after the second year.

In its first year a calf stag will develop knobs of bone on the skull. Known as pedicels, these will eventually carry the horns. In the second year the deer is known as a knobber. The third year is the pricket stage. From this point the horns continue to grow in length, weight and tines (points) until the seventh to ninth year when a full, classical head should have developed.

In the West Country the first three branches – the brow, bay and tray – are called the 'rights'. To count the points, a wedding ring is placed over each one. It's not valid if it can't hold the ring. So a set of horns with three points on both would be known as having 'all its rights and three atop'. Sometimes the stag's bay point may not develop until it is four years old but it would still be said to have its rights.

A good set of horns would have a sizeable beam (thickness) and the points would be long (three or four at least 7.5cm (3in) long and a good spread). The growth of the horns depends on the food and shelter available – as they are grown annually considerable nutrition is required.

Reader's top tips

DEER CONTROL

To keep deer out of your garden, collect unwashed human hair and fill a few small 'purses' made from discarded nylon tights. Hang them at appropriate places around the boundary fence. The deer should then find your garden wholly unattractive.

MR Warren, Lewes, Sussex

Stings from the Sea

Q. During recent holidays we have come across two creatures that, I am told, give an extremely painful sting. One is a weever fish and the other a Portuguese Man O' War. As we usually have a large crowd of young children with us I would like to know the best way of treating these stings immediately.

SS, York

A. The sting from both of these creatures is incredibly painful. The weever fish is a small, sandy-coloured fish that usually lies buried in the sand on the sea bed and is usually found at low tide. It has spines on its back that contain venom and, if trodden on, will sting. The pain is intense, lasting for about two hours. The foot may swell up and go red for a few days. To treat this sting remove any spines that have remained, then immerse the foot in very hot water (the hottest the victim can withstand), for 30 minutes to kill the venom. Children have very sensitive skin so be careful not to scald them. Remember to top up with hot water during that time. Treatment for a sting from a Portuguese Man O' War is similar but you are strongly advised to seek medical attention if certain symptoms are present. Although the sting is excruciatingly painful it may be accompanied by other more serious symptoms such as swelling, itching elsewhere on the body, wheezing, feeling faint, a fast heart rate, difficulty swallowing or a swollen face or mouth. If this is the case it is imperative to dial 999. Otherwise, treat the sting by bathing with vinegar, remove any tentacles from the area with sticky tape and submerge the wound in very hot water. It is advisable still to seek medical attention. Apparently detached tentacles and specimens that are washed up on shore can sting just as painfully as those in the water.

Bee Off

Q. Last summer a colony of bees took up residence in my attic. I have no wish to harm the squatters, but would like them to change address. They are dormant, for now. Is there a humane way of getting rid of them?

MC, Henley-on-Thames, Oxon

A. The ideal time to move bees is early to mid March when the population of the colony will be smaller than at other times and easier to manage.

Your local swarms officer will need to assess the site before any action is taken, but he is likely to suggest one of the following. If the colony is inaccessible he will remove the bees with a vacuum cleaner. They will be unharmed by this and the bag will serve as a temporary hive until the bees are transferred in to an apiary. If it is possible to enter the attic and the bees are in a hanging position, a basket will be placed underneath, the cones cut and placed in the basket and covered with a secure net and they will be removed to an apiary.

Reader's top tips

BEE-KEEPING

Cut the tops off some old, thick, woollen socks and use them as wrist guards if you are a beekeeper. Pull them over the wrist before pulling on your gloves – they serve as an extra barrier where bees usually attack.

John Turford, Goathland, N. Yorks

Encouraging Hedgehogs

Q. We have had two visiting labradors for a month. To our horror we found their favourite pastime was hedgehog rolling. We had no idea we had hedgehogs in the garden. We had always been told there weren't any because their main predator is the badger: are badgers predators of hedgehogs? And how can I encourage more hedgehogs back in to our garden?

BTA, Bishops Lydeard, Somerset

A. The badger is one of the hedgehog's main predators as it has claws that are long enough to reach the skin between the hedgehog's spine and strong enough to rip it open.

Hedgehogs are prone to hazards such as lawnmowers, garden ponds and, of course, roads. There has been a dramatic decline in hedgehog numbers and the British Hedgehog Preservation Society (BHPS) is running a programme to examine why.

Hedgehogs are the gardener's friends as they eat slugs, beetles and caterpillars. If you are using slug pellets make sure they are inaccessible to hedgehogs and remove the dead slugs daily.

To encourage hedgehogs into your garden the BHPS suggests leaving out food for them; a plain meat-based pet food and some dried cat food are ideal. If you have a problem with cats stealing the food then try some unsweetened muesli or Weetabix and a handful of raisins. Provide fresh water too. The BHPS also suggests putting dogs on leads for their evening walk if they prove to be hedgehog baiters.

Feeding Hedgehogs

Q. Our young son returned from school recently with the news that one of his friends had found a slightly injured hedgehog by the road-side which he and his parents were attempting to nurse back to health. There then followed a family debate about what a hedgehog house guest should be fed. Is the traditional offering of bread and milk really appropriate?

MM, Cheshire

A. Hedgehogs travel far and wide in search of their natural mixed diet of insects, worms, carrion, fallen fruit, seeds, and roots. Ideally, the food you give them should correspond to their natural diet as closely as possible. The idea that bread and milk are good for them is a common misconception. Such a diet is totally unnatural for a hedgehog and may even cause it harm. Tinned dog food is much more suitable.

Anyone handling a wild hedgehog should also be wary of fleas, which they carry in number.

From the Archives

The following appeared in *The Field* in November 1986.

HEDGEHOG RAMP

Q. Can anything be made to help hedgehogs climb out of cattle grids?

CAC

A. A ramp in one corner, up which the hedgehogs can climb, is needed. This can be made of stone aggregate and cement, about 4 to 6in wide, with a slope and a roughened or ribbed surface. Alternatively make one of small plank or 3cm (1¼in) thick board, covered with 1cm (½in) mesh wire or plastic netting, stapled to the underside, 10 to 15cm (4 to 6in) wide, and place in position against the wall of the cavity at one corner, with a slope of not more than 45 degrees, so that the animals can easily clamber out.

Joyful Flower

Q. I read recently about a hedgerowplant called Traveller's Joy. I find no mention of this in my old plant books. Any information would be appreciated.

LJB, Bishop Monkton, Yorks

A. Traveller's Joy, also called Old Man's Beard, is a wild clematis. It is a hardy climber and has green-white, vanilla-scented flowers from June to September. It changes in late September to fluffy seedheads and is found commonly on the edge of woods and in hedges. Butterflies and bees love its scented blooms and the seedheads provide food and nesting material. Apparently French beggars used clematis to irritate their skin and produce sores, in the hope of receiving more money. Clematis is also known as Poor Man's Friend and Boy's Bacca. This plant has been connected with the Devil and witches because it was thought to choke other plants to death. It has also been associated with the Virgin Mary and God because of its whiteness. The ideal time to plant Traveller's Joy is mid-autumn to early spring. Dig a deep hole (enough to bury 15cm (6in) of the stem below the surface); ideally the base of the plant should be in the shade to reduce the risk of clematis wilt. If this does occur, cut back the healthy wood close to the soil.

If the wilt recurs then the plant will need to be destroyed. In February prune all healthy plants to a foot high.

Why So Many Wasps?

Q. In the last fortnight we have killed over 40 queen wasps. Last year we hardly saw any wasps in our garden so why are there so many queens now? Is it true that each queen killed means one nest fewer?

TR, by e-mail

A. Last year was bad for wasps because a mild winter caused the queen wasps to emerge early from hibernation and a late cold spell killed them.

The sting in the tail is that we have had a cold winter this year and the queens are emerging at the right time.

Every queen has the potential to build a nest. She searches for a suitable site (an empty burrow, garden shed or roof space). Then she constructs a small paper nest from chewed wood, reeds or fencing which is mixed with saliva. Since dormant sperm has been stored from mating the previous summer, the queen can lay eggs. These hatch into sterile females called workers and they take over nest-building and larvae-feeding while the queen continues to lay.

At the end of the summer the queen lays eggs which produce drones (males), and fertile females, the next queens. These swarm out of the colony and mate. The males and nest die shortly afterwards and the only wasps left alive are the mated queens, who find a safe place to hibernate for the winter.

Slugs

Q. I read the query regarding slow-worms and their diet of slugs with interest. It made me wonder whether slugs have a purpose in the garden or whether they are just a common pest.

EMW, by e-mail

A. The only purpose I can find for garden slugs is to provide a diet for birds, slow-worms, hedgehogs, beetles, frogs and toads. One of the more common pests found in the garden, their voracious and unfussy appetite – attacking roots, fruit, vegetables and leaves – makes them the gardener's *bêtes noires*. Our moist climate and lack of extreme temperatures give Britain the dubious honour of being the slug capital of the world.

Slugs, which are hermaphrodites, breed all year round but most eggs are laid in March to April and September to October. Those laid in the spring hatch after three weeks whereas the autumn eggs overwinter before hatching. Each slug lays around 300 eggs in batches of 50 in crevices in the soil. Young slugs usually stay underground feeding on humus and seemingly lurk in wait for seedlings to be planted. As each cubic metre of our soil contains an average of 200 slugs it is worth planning to attack the slugs as early as possible in the growing year and to entice as many slug-eating creatures as you can.

Reader's top tips

SLUGS

It is a little-known fact that slugs, those meddling garden molluscs, are quite fond of a drink. Putting out half a grapefruit filled with beer is an effective and eco-friendly alternative to poison. The slugs will drown, but at least they will die happy.

Charnissay Gwyn, Humbie, East Lothian

Prolific Hares

Q. What is a hare's breeding cycle? How many young do they have and if more than one do they 'scatter' them over the field?

HD, Lewes, East Sussex

A. Female hares (does) can be prolific breeders being pregnant from February through to September. The famed 'boxing matches' relate to courtship; the doe is receptive to a mate for only a few hours during one day of her oestral cycle. The gestation period lasts for 42 days. Does can produce up to four litters of three or four a year. The young, known as leverets, are born fully furred with eyes open. Hares do not have burrows but make a small depression in the long grass, known as a form, and this is where the doe leaves her young. She returns once a day, after dusk, to suckle them for about five minutes. As the leverets grow they separate, only returning to the main nest to suckle before scattering again. They are usually fully weaned at four weeks.

A Puzzling Tree

Q. Please can you tell me why the monkey puzzle tree is so called?

PB, Bognor Regis, West Sussex

A. The Chile Pine (*Araucaria araucana*) or monkey puzzle tree is native to Chile and Patagonia where its seeds are eaten.

The tree was introduced into this country in 1795 but was not widely planted until 50 years later when it became popular as an ornamental and avenue tree. It attains a height of 30m (100ft) and its large staminate and ovulate cones are usually, but not always, borne on different trees. This is the only hardy *Araucaria* in this country and it prefers the milder regions.

As far as I can discover, its common name monkey puzzle tree is said to have originated in Cornwall where a joker said, 'It would puzzle a monkey to climb that tree.' Because there was as yet no common name for the tree, it became known as the monkey puzzler, which evolved to monkey puzzle.

Vaseline for Squirrels

Q. My garden is visited regularly by many birds – robins, all the tits and finches, nuthatches, dunnocks and many which give me a great deal of pleasure to watch. However I am plagued by squirrels that eat the seed, peanuts and fruitcake; apart from being so greedy they wreck the feeders. I've tried feeders inside cages and anti-squirrel pepper, which they seem to get used to after a while. Any other suggestions would be appreciated.

KJ, Swafield, Norfolk

A. Having suffered similarly, I can sympathise. We also tried the cage feeders and the pepper, to no avail. Then we tried one of the tall poles with double arms and sited it far enough from the bird-table and trees that the squirrels could not jump on to it – so they ran up the pole instead, despite the fact that it has a completely smooth and shiny surface. After watching them for a while we covered the pole generously with ordinary Vaseline and it worked. The squirrels would get half-way up the pole and start to slide down, which irritated them greatly. After about three weeks they stopped trying.

Some months later they had another go so we again applied Vaseline, and after about three weeks they gave up. You do have to apply the Vaseline frequently during the three-week period as a lot of it gets rubbed off by the squirrels and if they can get reasonable purchase to about half-way up they can manage to sort of skim up the rest of the pole despite the Vaseline.

We have found that the only seed and peanut feeders that survive squirrel attacks are those with stainless steel tops, bottoms, perches and mesh, and although expensive to buy they won't need replacing for a very long time, if ever.

Bats and Moles

Q. Can bats and moles swim?

NM

A. Bats can swim, although it is doubtful whether they ever do so except when they have accidentally fallen into streams or ponds over which they have been hawking. Moles swim quite well, using their large hand-like forepaws with powerful downward and backward strokes. When swimming the head and the front part of the body projects above the surface. We should doubt whether any British mammal is unable to swim.

Food for the Birds

Q. We always throw out any leftover bread for the birds, but can you suggest a good recipe for bird-cakes and advise what food we should put out on the bird-table?

PGB, Herts

A. Make up a mixture of seeds, nuts, dried fruits, oatmeal, cheese and cake in a large bowl. Melt some shredded suet (about one-third to two-thirds mixture) and stir in thoroughly until the ingredients bind well and can be made into small balls. Leave in a cool place to set. Wrap in large-meshed chicken wire and hang from a tree or bird-table.

Food for the bird-table could include finely chopped bacon rind, cooked rice (without salt), dry porridge oats, chopped up apples, sultanas and raisins.

Pecking Pudding

Q. Please can you give me a recipe for something fortifying to feed the tits in my garden ?

CM, Beckenham, Kent

A. Tie a knot in a length of hemp rope. Then, in a bowl, mix together a cup of crumbs (bread or cake), half a cup of sultanas, half a cup of millet or sunflower seeds, half a cup of oatmeal, quarter of a cup of chopped nuts and some bacon fat or cheese. To this add some melted suet – enough to bind the ingredients together – and when cool enough to handle, form into a ball around the knot. Roll the ball in sunflower seeds or millet and when completely cold, hang somewhere suitable, out of the reach of cats.

Encouraging Swallows

Q. I am converting a barn which should be finished by the end of April. It is inhabited by swallows every year and, as I enjoy having them around, I wonder if there is a way of persuading them to build on the exterior?

AS, by e-mail

A. Mike Everett of the RSPB tells me that you should try to have the barn fully sealed by mid-April as you can expect to start seeing swallows in the second or third week. They will spend about a week feeding to replenish fat reserves lost on their three-week journey from southern Africa. There will then be a rush to find a mate, build a nest and start breeding. With access to the barn denied, they will seek somewhere else. The best hope is to continue to allow access to the other buildings and to provide shelves or something similar within these, that replicate the lost site. However, swallows prefer to nest more or less inside, so are unlikely to choose an external nest-site.

Curried Eggs

Q. I have been keeping hens for while now and when I find an egg in an unusual place I wonder how long it has been there. Is there a way of telling how fresh an egg is? Also I have heard that curry powder is good for chickens. Is this true?

MHEF, Brockbridge, Hants

A. Put the egg into a glass of water. If it is fresh it will sink and lie on the bottom. If the egg is three weeks old, the broad end will just tilt up off the bottom; the higher the tilt the older the egg. At three months old, it will stand bolt upright with the broad end sitting just above the water level. If it rises much higher than this it is very stale indeed.

Domestic poultry have been known to develop a taste for curry powder and some people feed it regularly to their chickens, particularly during the winter months, say, November to January (a time when birds do not generally lay well) in order to perk them up and get them laying. Do not, however, use large amounts of curry powder as it will taint the eggs.

Flown the Nest

Q. This year, for the first time, we were lucky enough to have swallows nesting. Now that they have gone, is it better to leave their old nests in place or remove them so that they can build new ones?

JB, Aberfeldy, Perthshire

A. Leave the nests well alone. Swallows are creatures of habit and will return again and again to the same place. Sometimes they re-use a nest. In other years they may build a new one close by.

Is Bracken Dangerous?

Q. I understand that bracken is carcinogenic but only dangerous at certain times of the year when its spores are released. Do you know when these periods occur?

JDG, Bonby, Humberside

A. Bracken spores are known to be carcinogenic and in countries where croziers (the stem of baby plants) are eaten as a delicacy, there is a high rate of cancer. However, how the spores get into the human system has not yet been discovered.

Spores are released from the end of July into September but not every year and it is impossible to forecast which years they will appear. If you are working around bracken it would be a good idea to wear a dust filter.

Glowing in the Dark

Q. One evening last summer I noticed there were 20 or more glow-worms on our lawn. I did not mow the lawn until they had disappeared for fear of killing them. Are they nocturnal and, if they come back, will it be safe to mow this summer? I would also like to know more about these creatures.

MHEF, Hampshire

A. Glow-worms are not worms at all but beetles (*Lampyris noctiluca*). The adults can usually be seen from mid-June and mid-July when they emerge, mate, lay their eggs and die. The rest of their time is spent as egg, larva and pupa.

To attract a mate, the female will crawl to the top of a grass stem and sit with her light organs glowing, usually from around 10pm to midnight for up to 10 nights. These lights normally consist of two bands and two small spots towards the tip of the abdomen. The green glow is caused by a chemical reaction.

The males are smaller and have the light-producing spots but not the bands. The biggest difference, however, is that they have wings. The male flies within a metre or so of the ground scanning for a displaying female. Once spotted, it literally stops flying and falls with remarkable accuracy. After a successful mating, the eggs may be laid singly or in clusters, each one stuck down with a film of quick-drying glue. This will usually be close by, somewhere moist but not waterlogged, perhaps at the base of grass stems or in moss. The adults will be dead within a few days and do not see the eggs hatch.

The lawn can be mowed during the summer as the glow-worms are fairly safe at the base of the grass stems or underground. If you want to encourage them, do not remove slugs and snails as this is their main source of food. Their favourite habitat is weeds and long grass so, if at all possible, leave an uncultivated area in the garden.

Making a Killing

Q. For several weeks I watched a peregrine falcon living on top of the Stock Exchange which was very effective at keeping the pigeons at bay. When it left, a kestrel took over the post. Is it unusual to see such birds in cities?

KH, Reading

A. It is quite usual for peregrine falcons to roost on sheltered ledges on buildings in winter during the non-breeding season (this one had probably been resident at the Stock Exchange for some time).

They are attracted by the large number of pigeons which give them an easy source of food. In the spring they return to the countryside to breed. This behaviour is common throughout the UK and all over the world.

Kestrels do not sit comfortably with peregrines as the peregrine can sometimes make a meal out of the kestrel, but the fact that the kestrel took over the site was not necessarily connected with the peregrine's departure.

Sexing Lobsters

Q. I hear that hen lobsters are more fleshy than the cocks. However, when buying live lobsters, is it possible to tell the difference? And can you tell the difference between male and female crabs?

GMC, Winchester

A. Look under the lobster's tail; the top pair of small legs will be soft and flabby in a hen but made of hard shell in the cock. Crabs have a sort of flap under the body which is broad in a hen and narrow in a cock.

To pick up a live lobster or crab using your fingers, seize it by the back where the claws join the body, so that it cannot reach you. To remove a crab from a creel, get a good hold and lift out quickly, otherwise it will grip the sides of the creel with its legs and you will not be able to move it.

Catching the Egg Thief

Q. Earlier this year, in a wooded area at the bottom of my garden, I found a pheasant's nest containing six eggs, and over the following week three more appeared. One morning all nine had gone without trace. Can a predator remove eggs without damaging them?

JKR, Northumberland

A. Hedgehogs have been known to roll eggs away without breaking any, but possibly a stoat with a nest full of young might have taken them. A stoat can pick up pheasant, partridge or duck eggs using its four canine teeth without puncturing them.

Rising Tree Sap

Q. In September I noticed one of our very old oak trees had a dark, moist patch on just one section rising out of the ground. Where the trunk levelled out, the bark was covered in wasps and red admiral butterflies competing for a white froth which was apparent in minute quantities on the bark. What were they feeding on, and why were there only these two species?

J-MK, East Devon

A. The appearance of the white froth is known as sap-run and occurs in various species of trees. It is commonly found in horse chestnuts and more so in oaks, and is usually the result of some sort of internal injury, though the causes are not known.

When the sugars in the sap are exposed to the air they start to ferment, and give off gases which smell like over-ripe apples. Though the sap attracts all sorts of insects, wasps and red admirals particularly like its sweet taste.

This sap-run may occur only once or may persist for a number of weeks. On some trees it happens every spring and dries up in the summer. It is not a good sign, but neither does it mean that the tree is going to become diseased or die, so there is no need to chop it down.

Bird on the Wire

Q. My grandson climbed a laurel bush and came down with an old woodpigeon's nest. It felt unusually heavy and under close examination was found to have been constructed almost entirely of scraps of wire netting. Is this very unusual?

GMS, Ipswich

A. Generally birds use small twigs and sticks to make their nests, but often collect rags and paper which also make good nest-building materials.

Although unusual instances have been reported, such as a mistle-thrush which used shreds of plastic picked up from a local company's waste, and a crow which used fence wire, this is the first time the RSPB has heard of wire netting nest material and has added it to its 'unusual' list.

The Enemy Within

Q. We park our car close to the bird table outside the kitchen window. A tit has started perching on the wing mirror, looking at itself from different angles and then launching an attack. Is this behaviour unusual?

RCR, Hampshire

A. This type of behaviour is fairly common among tits, wagtails and chaffinches. Generally it is the territorial males which are attracted to their own reflection.

They can be seen puffing their feathers and squaring-up to the mirror, glass or hub-cap 'opponent', and often enter into quite severe physical fights. The birds become extremely frustrated because their adversary will not back down and, of course, the birds can never win the battle.

Of Harts and Hummels

Q. Can you enlighten me as to the meaning of the terms 'muckle hart', 'switch' and 'hummel'?

JB, Cheshire

A. A muckle hart is a Scottish term for a very large stag. A hummel is a stag that has no horns and for some reason is usually a heavier beast than most, and a switch is a stag which has only brow points or none at all, other than the sharp tines on the terminal branches.

If such a beast gets into a fight he can easily kill his opponent as the tines will be dagger-like and there are no points to 'lock' with the other stag's antlers.

Tickled Pink

Q. Can you tell me why the flesh of trout is pink?

KD, Kent

A. This is due to the trout's diet of crustaceans, such as shrimps, which, though not necessarily pink themselves, contain a pigment which works into the flesh when digested by the trout. Incidentally, farm-reared trout are fed pellets containing a pink dye to make them resemble their wild counterparts. White fish feed almost exclusively on insects and plankton.

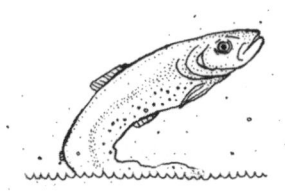

Starling Habits

Q. I am wondering if you can explain why starlings congregate in huge flocks in the treetops. They chatter very noisily for twenty to thirty minutes and then all depart together. Do they also do this in the UK?

DM, New Zealand

A. Many starlings come in from the continent to winter with ours and form these huge flocks. What you are witnessing is a sort of staging post; the starlings gather in the tops of trees or sometimes on buildings in towns, where it is a degree or two warmer. After chattering and calling others to join them for a while, they fly off in one large flock to form part of a main roost elsewhere, which may consist of thousands of birds.

It is interesting to note that your starlings in New Zealand behave in the same way as ours and have not changed their patterns of roosting despite differences in habitat and climate.

Counting Ladybirds

Q. My grandson's delight with nature is often the catalyst for an explosion of questions on the whys and wherefores of Mother Nature. Thankfully, many can be answered with ease but while walking through our local woods recently he demanded to know why there are no ladybirds in winter and why they have different numbers of spots. Can you help?

DS, Oxon

A. Ladybirds hibernate during the winter (sometimes in large groups) and emerge mostly in May and June although one or two species appear as early as March. Species vary widely in their colourings and markings.

For example, *Thea* 22-*punctata* has 22 black spots on a yellow background while *Scymnus frontalis* may be completely black with no spots at all. But the most common ladybird is *Coccinella* 7-*punctata* which is red with seven black spots.

Lucky Finds

Q. Having been fortunate enough to discover a four-leaved clover a while ago, I wondered if they are ever found with even more leaves than that?

TW, Durham

A. In most cases finding a four-leaved clover is still sufficiently uncommon to justify the expectation of good luck. The usual number is three, as the botanical name *Trifolium* implies, but abberations of up to seven have been found, each carrying a message for the impressionable.

Four leaves signify perfect harmony, five fame, six promises money and seven prosperity all one's life. In addition, a four-leaved clover is said to have the power to dissolve magic spells.

However, the discovery must be just that; since luck generally does not attend those who seek it deliberately. Make of that what you will, four-leaved versions have been found in most of the trefoils, including the shamrock, *Trifolium dubium* (which is especially lucky).

Evil-Eyed Peacocks

Q. Why are peacock feathers considered to be unlucky?

BRS, by e-mail

A. It is thought unlucky to decorate the home with peacock feathers because of the eye shape on the feathers. The eye is believed to be the 'evil eye' that is associated with wickedness.

In Greek mythology Hera gave Argus, a 100-eyed monster, the tasking of guarding Io, who was one of Zeus's many mistresses. However, on Zeus's orders, Hermes lulled Argus to sleep and then killed him.

Hera, distraught, took Argus's eyes and placed them on the feathers of her favourite bird, the peacock.

Picking off Ticks

Q. Since moving into Battle from a rural cottage, I have discovered that ticks are not just a country problem. From March, both our cat and dog came in with numerous small ticks on them. I then remembered reading in a past issue of *The Field* that ticks can breed in bracken and fern, of which there were several large clumps in the garden. We dug them out and I am pleased to say our tick days seem to be over, apart from the odd one brought home by the dog.

If you do remove ticks it is vital to get the head, as an abscess can form if it is left in. I found a dab of gin and tweezers was the answer to removal. Our animals regularly picked up ticks at our previous home and I became quite adept at removing them until our vet suggested spraying the tick with Nuvan Top flea spray. The tick then drops off of its own accord.

I should be interested to learn where the ticks could have originated from as there were no sheep in our garden.

RCB, East Sussex

A. Ticks can be left by deer and cattle as well as sheep and possibly this is where they came from. It is true that it is important to remove the heads and the only way I know of doing this is to use Nuvan Top or methylated spirits – gin I have yet to try.

Reader's top tips

TICKS

To remove ticks from your dog, dab them with some neat Dettol antiseptic. The ticks will soon fall off dead.

Paul McNally, Tyne and Wear

Dietary Debate

Q. There is a debate running in my family as to whether it is harmful to feed our spaniel too many vegetables. Is it inadvisable to feed them to dogs, and are certain vegetables of better dietary value than others?

DW, Oxfordshire

A. There is no objection to feeding sporting dogs small quantities of green vegetables, although they are not too easily digested and can often give a dog wind. The dog is a carnivorous animal primarily, so at least 50 per cent of its ration should be of either meat or fish. Generally speaking, slops, porridge and so on should be avoided and the food should be dry. Other foods to be avoided are uncooked slaughterhouse offal, uncooked rabbit, uncooked bones, fish-bones, poultry and rabbit or game-bird bones.

It is possible to feed dogs on a vegetarian diet. For meat protein, substitute milk products, cheese and eggs and the proteinous vegetables such as soya beans, legumes and whole-grain cereals. Potatoes are not rich in protein, but can be served whole.

There are some excellent proprietary dried foods on the market, but ask your vet which one he recommends. Remember also that dogs should be given ample chewy material in their diet.

Reader's top tips

SMELLS

When your dog has rolled in a fox or badger's calling card get rid of the smell by rubbing its coat with ketchup, then rinsing.

C David, Notts

Dog Biscuits

Q. May I have a recipe for dog biscuits so I can make them myself?

BW, Kent

A. Stir together in a bowl 1.3kg (3lb) whole-wheat flour, 450g (1lb) self-raising flour, 450g (1lb) maize or cornmeal, 225g (½lb) wheat bran, 450g (1lb) finely minced lean beef, one tbs each of tomato juice or purée, cod-liver oil, and bonemeal, with sufficient stock, milk or water to make a stiff dough.

Roll out dough until it is 1cm (½in) thick, cut into biscuit shapes, and place on a greased baking sheet. Bake for about an hour in a slow oven.

Sporting Lore and History

Drinking Song

Q. My father, who was born in Northamptonshire in 1892, used to sing a lively hunting song. I believe that part of the chorus went, 'So drink, puppy, drink, let every puppy drink... and we'll all halloo and we'll follow.' I wonder whether any *Field* readers might know this song as I would love to know all the words.

EMM, Chipping Norton, Oxon

A. *Drink, Puppy, Drink* was a song composed by the novelist George John Whyte-Melville, who lived from 1821 to 1878.

The words are as follows:

Here's to the fox in the earth below the rocks,

And here's to the line that we follow,

And here's to the hound with his nose upon the ground,

Tho'merrily we whoop and we holloa!

Chorus (after every verse):

Then drink, puppy, drink,

Let every puppy drink,

That's old enough to lap and to swallow,

For he'll grow into a hound,

So we'll pass the bottle round,

And merrily we'll whoop and we'll holloa.

Here's to the horse and to the rider, too, of course,

And here's to the rally o'the hunt, boys;

Here's a health to every friend, who can struggle to the end,

And here's to the tally-ho in front, boys.

Here's to the gap and the timber that we rap,

Here's to the white thorn, and the black, too;

And here's to the pace that puts life into the chase,

And the fence that gives a moment to the pack, too.

Oh, the pack is staunch and true,

Now they run from scent to view,

And it's worth the risk to life and limb and neck, boys;

To see them drive and stoop till they finish with 'Who-whoop',

Forty minutes on the grass without a check, boys,

Poetry Please

Q. I am trying to find the wording of a poem which I know as 'Logs for Burning'. The version I know has a line: 'ash logs green as being fit for a queen'. Could you help me in tracing it?

RS, Cold Aston, Gloucestershire

A. I have located a poem translated from Latin which appeared as a letter in *The Times* in 1929:

Beechwood fires are bright and clear if the logs are kept a year.

Chestnut's only good, they say, if for long it's laid away.

Make a fire of elder tree, death within your house shall be.

But ash new or ash old is fit for a queen with a crown of gold.

Birch and fir logs burn too fast; blaze up bright and do not last.

It is by the Irish said, hawthorn bakes the sweetest bread.

Elm wood burns like a churchyard mould; e'en the very flames are cold.

But ash green or ash brown is fit for a queen with a golden crown.

Poplar gives a bitter smoke, fills your eyes and makes you choke.

Apple wood will scent your room with an incense-like perfume.

Oaken logs, if dry and old, keep away the winter cold

But ash wet or ash dry a king shall warm his slippers by.

Euston to Portree

Q. The query about *Going North, Coming South* in the January issue reminded me of a poem I saw many years ago but don't know where. It was about a chap on Euston station who sees another chap with his dogs, guns and rods 'proudly labelled for Portree'. That is all I can remember and have no clue as to where to look. Can you help?

JW, Corston, Wiltshire

A. Lines penned *At Euston (by one who is not going)* by A M Harbord:

Stranger with the pile of luggage proudly labelled for Portree
How I wish this night of August I were you and you were me!
Think of all that lies before you when the train goes sliding forth
And the lines athwart the sunset lead you swiftly to the North!
Think of breakfast at Kingussie, think of high Drumochter Pass.
Think of highland breezes singing through the bracken and the grass.
Scabious blue and yellow daisy, tender fern beside the train
Rowdy tummel falling, brawling, seen and lost and glimpsed again!
You will pass my golden roadway of the days of long ago:
Will you realise the magic of the names I used to know;
Clachnaharry, Achnashellash, Achnasheen and Duirinish?
Ev'ry moor alive with coveys, ev'ry pool aboil with fish;
Every well remembered vista more exciting by the mile
Till the wheeling gulls are screaming round the engine at the Kyle
Think of cloud on Bheinn na Cailleach, jagged Cuillins soaring high
Scent of peat and all the glamour of the misty Isle of Skye!
Rods and gun case in the carriage, wise retriever in the van;
Go and good luck travel with you! (Wish I'd half your luck, my man!)

Auld Handsel Monday

Q. Can you please settle an argument and tell me what to be 'handselled' means and whether it relates to New Year's Day or another date?

NSB, Nettlestead, Suffolk

A. Handsel means giving into the hands; particularly the sale, gift or delivery into the hand of another that is the first in a series and is regarded as an omen for the rest; the first instalment on something, the first money taken at a market or fair of a morning, or the first present sent to a bride on her wedding day.

Handsel Monday is the first Monday in the year and was generally regarded as an occasion for universal tipping. Until the early 20th century it was a holiday festival in Perthshire and much more celebrated than New Year's Day.

These days, to handsel generally means to give a coin for good fortune on Handsel Monday, particularly to children, although this custom is not as widespread as it once was. A related custom is that of putting money into a purse or wallet that is being given as a present. I remember as a child being given a purse that had a shiny penny inside, but since decimalisation and with the value of money today perhaps a £1 coin might be more appropriate, or even one of the variety of £5 coins now available.

Ticketed Pink

Q. The other day at lunch, a friend said she had given her husband a 'pink ticket'. She explained the phrase meant that he could have the evening out without her but she had no idea where the expression came from. Can you enlighten us?

SF, London

A. Cdr Melvin Anderson, who joined the Navy in 1965, believes it is a derivative of the 'brown card'. For much of the 20th century Naval leave was based on a colour-coded card system. A ship's company was divided into two watches. The port watch held red cards and the starboard watch green. The Quartermaster standing duty on the gangway permitted or denied a sailor leave depending on which watch was on duty.

Those who were allowed to go ashore at any time held a brown card. This was, in effect, a free pass to come and go as the holder pleased and it is a short step from the brown card to the pink ticket.

This ties in with *Covey Grump*, a collection of Naval slang and historical titbits, which defines the pink ticket as the metaphorical card of permission obtained by a married officer from his wife to enable him to join in an evening's entertainment at which she will not be present.

To Coventry

Q. Could you tell me the origin of the phrase 'to send someone to Coventry' please?

MSC, Pershore, Worcs

A. According to Brewer's *Dictionary of Phrase and Fable*, the citizens of Coventry once had so great a dislike of soldiers that a woman seen speaking to one was instantly outlawed. Hence when a soldier was sent to Coventry he was cut off from all social intercourse. Edward Hyde, Earl of Clarendon, in his *History of the Great Rebellion* (1702–4), says that Royalist prisoners captured in Birmingham were sent to Coventry, which was a Parliamentary stronghold.

Cold Comfort

Q. In the grounds of our local golf course is an old ice house. The entrance to it has been filled in for safety reasons and until recently it simply looked like an overgrown hill. The brick chimney has fallen but we plan to clear the area and have the chimney re-sited. Could you tell us the history of ice houses?

DL, by e-mail

A. The tradition of building ice houses seems to have begun in the late 17th century; by the 18th century, no estate would be without one. At this time they were usually built as a brick-lined pit or chamber, square, circular or cone-shaped with a length or diameter of 2m (6ft) to 4m (12ft) and vertical sides up to 10m (30ft) deep. A domed structure was then built on top with a passage leading to a north-facing entrance sheltered by trees. The passages were usually straight but some were built with one or more right-angled turns to prevent warm air and sunlight getting into the chamber and some had two doors to provide an air-lock. But by the end of the 18th century the general opinion was that damp, dark conditions were not good for the preservation of ice; also, the height of the underlying water table made efficient drainage of melted ice difficult. So partially buried or above-ground ice houses in light, airy locations were recommended and the more complex ones were built with double or cavity walls that were packed with charcoal, straw or stone to help with insulation. Thus ice houses can be found in a wide variety of designs.

Ice houses were often on the margins of an estate where ice could be collected from small, shallow ponds, taken to the ice house and there compressed into one large block. By the 19th century, the location of the ice house was less important as ice became available from commercial suppliers, either imported or collected from ice works. The ice was transported in blocks and stacked between layers of straw on wooden shelves. Ice began to be imported from Norway in the 1820s and large ice wells were dug at 12–13 New Wharf Road, London N1 (now the London Canal Museum) in order to store ice to meet the growing demand from restaurants, fishmongers and others who wanted it to keep food chilled. This mass import reduced the price sufficiently to allow the manufacture of ice-cream for sale to the general public. The ice arrived by ship at Regent's Canal Dock (now called Limehouse Basin) in East London and was taken by horse-drawn barges on Regent's Canal to the ice wells which were in use until at least 1902. The last import of any ice from Scandinavia was in 1921, by which time mechanical ice production was well established.

The London Canal Museum has an exhibition on the import of ice and is open weekly, Tuesday to Sunday, tel 020 7713 0836; or visit www.canalmuseum.org.uk.

Riding a Bumper Race

Q. With reference to racing, can you tell me what a 'bumper' is?

CN, Sevenoaks, Kent

A. A bumper is a flat race run at the end of a National Hunt meeting for four, five, or six- and occasionally seven-year-old jumping horses to gain experience. Under Jockey Club Rules they must not have run in any flat races other than NH flat races in Great Britain and not more than four Irish NH flat races.

Some people think that the word 'bumper' refers to the horses bumping into each other because they are novices on the flat. In fact, it refers to the jockeys who were originally amateurs, though professionals are now eligible. Many amateurs are untidy riders and often bump around in the saddle – hence the nickname.

... *From the Archives* ....

The following appeared in *The Field* in June 1900.

TIGER BOY

Q. Can you clarify the occupation of a Tiger Boy?

LMM

A. The term 'tiger', as applied to a boy acting as carriage groom, is now seldom heard. When the cabriolet was a common vehicle, it was customary for a small boy to stand on the platform behind. The word tiger is said to have arisen from the stripes on the waistcoat that was commonly worn.

... *Reader's top tips* ....

HORSES

To keep your horses' tails shiny and tangle-free just spray with cheap furniture polish before brushing.

Sue McConnel, Oxfordshire

Ensure New Year Luck

Q. Every year there's confusion in our house about who should cross the threshold first at midnight at New Year and what they should be carrying. Can you clarify the details?

NB, Portchester, Hampshire

A. According to the *Hogmanay Companion* by Hugh Douglas, the first footer, who is said to bring good luck for the forthcoming year, should be a dark-haired, healthy man. He must not be a minister, doctor or grave-digger and should be honest, good-tempered and liked by all.

The first footer must not carry a sharp tool with him, but must bring a piece of coal to signify warmth and comfort, cake to denote plenty, a silver coin to ensure prosperity and a bottle – preferably whisky – to toast the health of all who live in the house.

Ponds Long Over Dew

Q. I recently moved to the Peak District and have come across what the locals call a dew pond. Can you tell me what dew ponds are, their origins and their use today?

Cd R, Bakewell, Derbyshire

A. Dew ponds, or rain ponds, were man-made watering holes for livestock, usually sited at the bottom of a hill or an incline. Their effectiveness as a source of water depended on the soundness of their structure and freedom from leaks.

The earth was scooped out to make shallow, saucer-shaped hollows, the greatest depth – about a tenth of the diameter of the pond – being at the centre. The bottom of the pond would be lined with 10 to 15cm (4 to 6in) of well-packed straw; a 20cm (8in) layer of puddled clay; and finally a hard layer of mortar. The rim of the pond would be studded with large boulders, referred to as condenser stones.

Dew ponds were made until about a hundred years ago when they went out of fashion as piped water and troughs were introduced. Over the years they were used as the village tip or filled in with rubbish and overgrown with vegetation.

The Tale of St George

Q. Why did St George slay the dragon? I realise both figures are probably mythical, but I have been unable to find out the entire story.

HJP, Co Tipperary

A. St George was of Greek origin and lived in the third century AD. He was a soldier in the Roman army and was executed on the order of Emperor Diocletian on 23 April 303 for refusing to renounce Christianity.

The legend goes that while St George was travelling in the Middle East, he arrived in a kingdom near Lydda just as the king's daughter was about to be handed over to a wicked dragon.

St George slew the dragon and rescued the princess. The king was so overjoyed that he offered his daughter's hand to St George as a reward for his bravery. However, he turned down the king's proposal and continued his journey.

St George has since been regarded as the most chivalrous of knights. His banner, the Crusader's cross, has been worn by English soldiers for centuries. The mythical tale of his dragon-slaying led him to become the patron saint of England, Aragon and Portugal.

Are We April Fools?

Q. Can you possibly tell me why April Fool's Day is so called?

JB, Nottingham

A. In classical Rome the year began on 1 January, but in the Middle Ages, under Christian influences, other dates were chosen. From the late-12th century, New Year celebrations started on the Feast of the Annunciation (Lady Day), 25 March. People would hold parties and give presents from then until 1 April.

In 1751 Lord Chesterfield's Act reformed the calendar to start the year on 1 January. But many people either refused to accept this or did not know it had happened. As they continued to hold parties and give presents from 25 March to 1 April, they were mocked, sent daft gifts, had tricks played upon them and were nicknamed April Fools.

What a Hoot

Q. Can you tell me what the terms owlers and owling mean?

LF, London

A. Owlers were wool smugglers and were thought to look like owls when they carried wool or sheep on their backs at night. A favourite place for smuggling wool to France was Romney Marsh, and fast vessels which slipped out of the creeks in Sussex were known as owling boats.

Owling, however, is completely unrelated, It refers to the now illegal practice of tethering an owl in daylight to a frame which has twigs covered in bird lime attached to it. Other birds would then attack the owl, become trapped by the bird lime and then be captured.

Prickly Bounty

Q. In our churchwarden's accounts from the early 19th century there are records showing the sum of 4d being paid for killing two hedgehogs in the churchyard. This seems a high price compared to a record showing 6d for digging a grave. Why and when did the killing of hedgehogs begin?

DBW, South Glamorgan

A. Hedgehogs were once considered vermin and used to be destroyed. The payments were similar to those in more recent times for rat and squirrel tails, crows and so on.

The practice of paying a bounty for a dead hedgehog started in 1559 during the reign of Queen Elizabeth I who passed a law decreeing that threepence was to be paid for every hedgehog killed as they, along with rats and mice, damaged crops.

Forrtunately for the hedgehog, this law was repealed in 1863.

St Swithin's Soaking

Q. St Swithin's Day on 15 July will supposedly herald 40 days of rain or 40 days of fine. What is the origin of this belief?

JDB, Leicester

A. It was a humble monk St Swithin. who suggested that he should be buried where the rain would fall on him. He was buried thus in 862 AD but in 971 AD it was thought that a more appropriate burial place for one of his godliness was Winchester Cathedral and an attempt was made to move him. It is said that his spirit was so outraged that it made it rain for the next 40 days.

Wedding Rhymes

Q. Everyone knows the rhyme, Something old, something new and so on, but what is each line meant to represent?

MF, Cheshire

A. Observing this rhyme is thought to ensure good fortune for the wedding day and throughout married life. Something old symbolises good influences from the past, something new signifies the new life ahead, and something is borrowed in the hope of friends' continuing loyalty.

Something blue represents constancy and loyalty. A sixpence in her shoe is for future wealth.

Field of Lightning

Q. Many years ago a friend of mine was told by an old black gentleman who worked on a tobacco plantation in the USA that should he ever get caught out in a lightning storm, the best place to shelter is under a beech tree. Apparently they are the only trees that never get struck. Do you know if there is any truth in this theory?

CFB-H, Inverness-shire

A. There are records showing that people and cattle have been killed while sheltering under beech trees; it is in fact dangerous to shelter under any tree during a storm. If you are unable to get inside a building, the best advice is probably to go into the middle of a field and lie face down.

Perhaps the theory you quote stems from the way beech trees often respond to lightning strike. Trees with a smooth bark, such as beech, are covered with a film of water through which the lightning is conducted, often producing only minimal signs of damage such as the death of a few leaves. Conversely, the water film may not be complete over the surface of a tree with rough bark (such as oak), so that the discharge of electricity causes the water in the wood to boil producing enormous damage.

Horse Chestnut Cure

Q. I have heard that horse chestnuts can be used as a remedy for curing ailments in horses. Is there any truth in this?

RW, South Glamorgan

A. The horse chestnut (*Aesculus hippocastanum*), whose native home is the mountainous, inaccessible wilds of Albania and Northern Greece, was known to the Turks who used the fruits as a drug. Ground down and mixed with oats they would administer small amounts to horses suffering from broken wind or a cough. Modern vets, however, do NOT advocate the use of this remedy.

The tree was first introduced to France in 1615 through seeds brought over from Constantinople and was probably introduced into England at the same time. Apparently gypsies superstitiously used to hang horse chestnuts on the saddles of their horses in order to ward off colds and coughs.

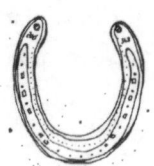

Cure for Rheumatism

Q. I have heard that juniper berries are useful for curing rheumatism. Is this true and how does one use the berries?

ACN, Sussex

A. Juniper is said to be good for arthritis and chronic rheumatism. It may be an old wives' tale, but to try the following infusion or 'wine' will do no harm and may do you a lot of good.

The berries of the juniper bush remain green for the first two years and should only be picked in their third year when they have turned a bluish-black in October/November. Wash the berries and then dry them in the open air, turning frequently. To make an infusion, add 30 to 40g (1 to 1¼oz) of crushed berries to a litre (1½ pints) of boiling water, leave for 10 minutes and strain. Three cupfuls should be taken daily.

To make a wine, add 50 to 60g (2to 2¼oz) of crushed berries to a litre (1½ pints) of white wine. Leave to macerate for 15 days, stirring occasionally. Then strain and sweeten to taste with honey. Drink one or two glassfuls during the day, well before or after meals.

Rainbow Rhetoric

Q. I was intrigued to hear that a rainbow in the west signifies light rain but one in the south means a heavy rainstorm is on its way. Do you know the origin of this wives' tale?

RY, London

A. The rainbow, associated with the supernatural, has been the subject of many legends. The originator of your wives' tale would seem to be Seneca, the Roman rhetorician.

A well-known nautical rhyme runs:

Rainbow in the morning, sailors take warning

Rainbow at night, sailor's delight

Rainbow to windward, foul fall the day

Rainbow to leeward, damp runs away.

Shove Ha'penny

Q. I aquired a Shove Ha'penny board recently. Can you tell me the rules of this game, and anything of its history?

JL, by e-mail

A. Shove Ha'penny has also been known as shovel-board, shove-groat, slide-groat and slip-groat. The 15th century groat was ideal in size and weight. Groats were replaced in the 16th century by shillings, and later the Victorian ha'penny proved equally suitable. Modern coinage is not so suitable, so it would be better to track down some old ha'pennies.

Royalty are known to have indulged in the game as the household accounts of Henry VII show when, in 1532, a gambling debt was paid, and Shakespeare alludes to it in *Henry IV Part II*, when Falstaff tells Bardolf to toss Pistol downstairs: 'Quoit him down, Bardolf, like a shove-groat shilling!' It was a favourite game of the landed gentry who had exquisite boards made for their country houses. When billiards became fashionable shove ha'penny declined. Today it is mostly played in pubs.

How to play: The board has nine horizontal 'beds', each having a scoring square on either end. The object is to shove a coin so that it falls within the borders of one of the nine beds. The two players, each having five coins, take it in turns to 'shove' and the first to score three coins in each of the nine beds is the winner. To shove a coin, place it on the bottom end of the board so that a portion sticks out over the edge. Then strike the coin with the palm of the hand or ball of thumb sending it up the board.

There are various rules about coins that land beyond the beds, on lines between beds, short of the first bed and coins that land on top of each other.

Lucky Rabbits

Q. Can you tell me why we say 'white rabbits' on the first day of each month, and does it bring luck?

BG, East Anglia

A. The rabbit was the symbol of the moon according to old Sanskrit literature, and this could be the origin of saying the word rabbits on the first day of a new month, at one time associated with the lunar month.

The association of rabbits and luck may stem from when it was said that young rabbits were born with their eyes open and so had power over the evil one and could ward off the evil eye in the same way as brasses on a horse harness. Similarly, it is thought that white symbolises good.

Some people say the word hares last thing at night on the eve of the month and then do not speak until they have said the word rabbits the following morning. Strangely though, fishermen and sailors believe the word rabbits to be unlucky.

Sign of Saint James

Q. Can you explain why the French name for scallops is *Coquilles Saint Jacques?*

BM, London

A. The scallop shell was worn by pilgrims who visited the shrine of Saint James of Compostella and owes its name to a local legend.

During a marriage celebration in the village of Bonzas, on the coast of Portugal, the bridegroom and some friends were riding along the shore when the bridegroom's horse became unmanageable and plunged into the sea. A passing ship, travelling without sails or oars, which was carrying the body of Saint James from Joppa to Galicia, appeared to stop and presently the bridegroom and horse emerged close beside it.

During the ensuing conversation between the groom and the saint's disciples, they told him that Saint James had saved him from a watery grave and explained the Christian religion to him. He believed and was baptised by the disciples.

The ship resumed its voyage and the groom galloped back over the sea to rejoin his astonished friends. When he told them what had happened, his friends were also converted, and he baptised his bride with his own hand.

On emerging from the sea, the groom's dress and horse's trappings were covered with scallop shells. Thus the Galacians took the scallop shell as the sign of Saint James.

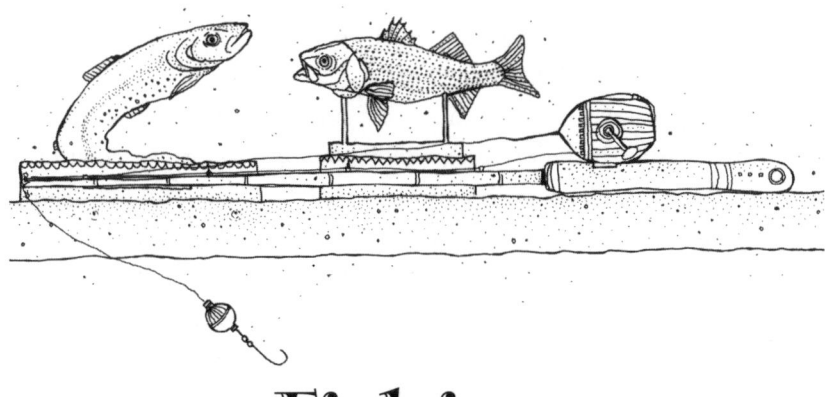

Fishing

How to Weigh a Trout

Q. I am a catch-and-release fisherman. There seem to be a number of ways to estimate the weight of a trout; please could you advise the best method?

TRPD, Hassocks, West Sussex

A. Well-known chalkstream angler and research specialist Peter Hayes tells me that several methods have been established over the years. Edward Sturdy published a trout table in the *Fishing Gazette* in the early twenties ranging from 9in=5oz to 26in=7lb 8oz.

Then there is the Alaska formula handed down by word of mouth from guide to guide: length to end of tail (inches) x girth (inches) squared, divided by 700=weight (pounds). Hayes says this formula tends to underestimate slightly. The most up to date and accurate formula comes from Ally Gowans and his son Dr Andy Gowans, which although it was developed for salmon, seems to work reasonably well for trout: (Kg)=41.4

—199—

x length x girth squared (length and girth in metres) The girth should be measures at the front of the dorsal fin.

Dr Gowans carried out a research project in 1994 on the Tay in which a range of statistics including measurements and weight, was collected from 875 fresh Tay salmon. Ally Gowans tested the formula for calculating weight published in *The Fisherman's Vade Mecum* by G W Maunsell in 1933 on the 875 fish and found that the weights were underestimated by it. They produced a new formula (as above) statistically corrected to mini-mise error; this new formula produced over 80 per cent of fish weights that were within 5 per cent of their actual weight.

Use a soft tape measure on live fish or failing that some tippet, nylon or string and cut a piece to the fish's length and another to its girth and measure them. Use the Gowans' formula (as above) or visit their website and put your figures into the calculator, www.letsflyfish.com/weight. htm. *See also* From the Archives, below.

From the Archives

The following appeared in *The Field* in March 1899.

WEIGHTS OF FISH

Estimating the weights of fish: the following is the rule for calculating the weight of salmon, trout and grayling. To the length of the fish from eye to tail-fork in inches, add one-third. Multiply the sum by the square of the girth, also in inches, and divide by 1,000. The quotient is the weight in pounds.

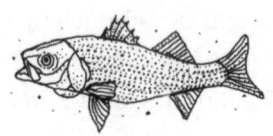

Fish on the Road

Q. I fish each year on South Uist. My return from Wales involves a seven-hour ferry crossing and a seven-hour car journey. What is the best way of transporting trout which has already been frozen and fresh trout hopefully caught on the last day, in my car?

PNN, Yns Mon, Wales

A. The best solution would be to pack the frozen fish in plenty of ice in a cool box and then pick up some fresh ice after the ferry journey, or ask someone on the ferry shortly before docking. I do know someone who brought salmon back from Alaska this way and it survived, although it had been vacuum-packed before being frozen.

Vacuum-packing extends the keeping life of fresh or frozen fish because there is no oxygen to cause changes in colour and flavour as well as loss of weight, and food will look and taste fresher. It does not, however, inhibit bacterial growth and food must still be kept chilled or frozen. If the hotel where you stay cannot do this, perhaps you should treat yourself to a Magic Vac to take on your travels. It is certainly compact enough to stick in the boot of your car. It could also be used at home for fresh or cooked meat, cheese, fruit and vegetables.

The smallest version of the Magic Vac is the Elite and packaging rolls come in packs of two that are 6m (20ft) in length and 20cm or 30cm (8in or 12in) wide. Contact Rusco Vac, Little Faringdon Mill, Lechlade, Gloucestershire GL7 3QQ, tel 01367 252754.

Reader's top tips

FLY-FISHING

If your fly gets stuck in a tree, reel all line and leader until the top ring touches the fly, then give a little twist.

Stan Yates, Darwen, Lancashire

Trout in the Dark

Q. The sea-trout season is approaching and soon I will be out at night fishing for them.

I usually have to tie on a new fly, untangle the leader and so on. If I were to use an infrared bulb would the fish see it too?

JNY, Winchester, Hants

A. Dr Richard Shelton, a fisheries expert, tells me that the fish wouldn't be able to see an infrared bulb, but neither would you. Infrared rays are reflected, refracted, absorbed and transmitted just like visible light but are invisible to the human eye, as are many other parts of the electromagnetic spectrum, such as gamma and radio waves.

The primary source of infrared is heat or thermal radiation and any object that has a temperature above absolute zero Fahrenheit radiates in the infrared. Humans at normal body temperature radiate the most strongly.

If you were to point an infrared beam at your hands tying a fly, you would see your hands moving in shades of red but it would be difficult to see the fly and line. It is thought that light that we can see, can also be seen by fish. However, experience shows that fish are less sensitive to light at the red end of the spectrum; therefore using a subdued red light would be better than one of any other colour.

···· *Reader's top tips* ································

SINKANT

A useful tip for trout fishermen: rather than spending a lot of money on expensive leader sinkants you can make your own by adding a small amount of washing-up liquid to some Fuller's Earth.

Rob Fletcher, Ruskie, Stirling

From the Archives

The following appeared in *The Field* in May 1952.

COCK OR HEN?

Q. How can one differentiate between cock and hen of brown trout?

NG

A. With small trout it is rather difficult to distinguish between cock and hen fish, but in sizes of 450g (1lb) and upwards the difference can be seen fairly easily by the following features: the head, measured from the eye to the tip of the nose is longer and larger in the male, which also has larger fins. In the male the gill cover is pointed, and in the female it is more rounded. The body of a cock looks longer, has less depth of body and is broader across the shoulder. The hen is deeper and more shapely. The belly: between the vent and the pectoral fin the cock fish is rather narrow, flat, square and hard, while the hen is broad, softer and rounded. In colour the cock has more and brighter spots and is more slimy to handle: it also has often a golden tint, while the hen is silvery.

Reader's top tips

GRIP THAT ROD

On wet days the handle of the rod can get slippery, so put a couple of elastic bands around it.

S Yates, Darwen, Lancashire

A Sticky Problem

Q. The widow of a fishing friend has given me four silk lines that are a little sticky. Can you tell me how to restore and dress these sound old lines?

KH, by e-mail

A. The following solution is from *Fisherman's Knots and Wrinkles* by W A Hunter dated 1927. 'To Cure a Tacky or Sticky Line: When the dressing of a waterproofed line has become tacky it can be completely cured in the following very simple manner. Make a loose coil of the line as large in diameter as will go into a soup plate or shallow basin: cover the line with lime-water (which can be bought cheaply at any chemist's) and separate the strands with your fingers so that the liquid reaches every inch of line surface. Two or three hours in this bath will generally suffice if the line is occasionally moved about in case any strands are still adhering to others, but it may be left in the bath all night without any ill effect. Shake all loose liquid from the coil and hang it up to dry when it will be found quite free from stickiness and only requiring rubbing down with "Mucilin" to remove the slight chemical deposit and revive the surface. Persistent rubbing (a foot or two at a time) will well repay the labour, but very little of the grease should be left on the line at the completion of the cure. We once tried this cure on an oilskin coat in an almost solid condition; it was only with great difficulty that the bundle was opened out into the semblance of a garment but after a night in the lime-water bath the coat was wearable again.'

I have also heard that petrol used sparingly, will suffice for stubborn lines.

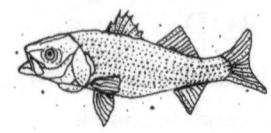

Muddy Trout

Q. The trout I catch in my local stream sometimes have a muddy taste. There is no muddy smell when the fish is raw and therefore no way of knowing whether it is a muddy one or not. Is there a way of ridding the fish of this muddy flavour – should it be present – prior to cooking?

AJH, Gillingham, Dorset

A. First clean your trout thoroughly and then soak it in a strong solution of salted water – at least 1 tablespoon per half litre (18fl oz) – for a good hour or two. This should remove all the muddy flavour. If you want to cook it straight away and don't have time to spare, clean it thoroughly, scald in boiling salted water, dry, and then cook. The second method may not remove the muddy flavour completely, but it should certainly lessen it.

Hook, Line and Needle

Q. Why is Worcestershire the centre of the fish-hook manufacturing industry?

LJ, Middlesex

A. A party of medieval monks who were skilled needle-makers settled in Redditch. Needles to fish hooks was a small step. When the South Seas were opened up to trade by Captain Cook and others a successful industry was born supplying the hooks to nations dependent upon fish for food.

So it continued for more than one hundred years but interruptions such as the two world wars meant that their customers started to produce hooks locally and now there are few manufacturers left in Redditch.

Recycling Flies

Q. Do old trout flies have any use?

ME, Devon

A. Old sea-trout flies are of no practical value, as the gut on which they are dressed will have perished. For anyone who ties his own flies, however, it is possible to make use of the wings.

With a sharp kitchen knife make a cut right through the head of the fly underneath and parallel to the hook. The whole wing, which is held together by the silk and varnish can then be lifted clear of the hook.

Remove the old gut without disturbing the feathers and then place the 'saddle' formed by the old head over an eyed hook on which you have previously tied a body, tail and hackle of the appropriate pattern. Take a couple of turns of tying silk over the roots of the wings immediately behind the original turns, and, having made sure the wings cannot slip, scrape off the old head with a knife. Form a new head and varnish.

Reader's top tips

NAIL

Put a 10cm (4in) nail, without the point, at the base of your rod handle. You can then place your rod upright in the ground when tying on a fly.

Stan Yates, Darwen, Lancashire

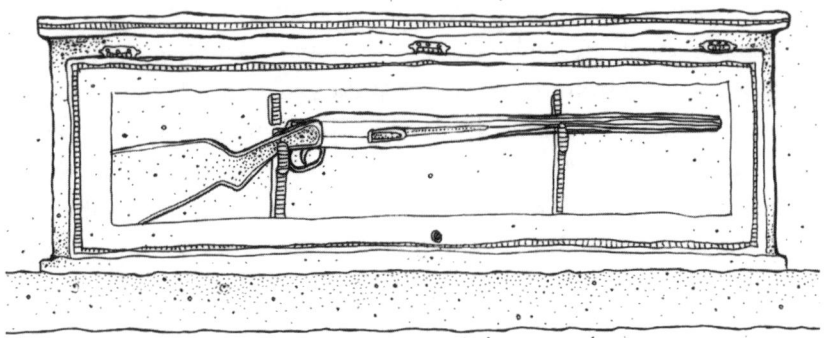

Shooting

Sharing Pegs

Q. I recently joined a 100-bird day shoot. After the second day of four I asked what the etiquette was for sharing a peg. This caused a huge debate, mostly negative. It seemed common practice to give your place to another gun if you were unavailable but sharing a peg seemed to be frowned upon. My guest had shot clays for many years but was inexperienced with game and I hoped to familiarise him. Lunch is out of the back of the car, so there is no problem with the ninth chair at a sit-down lunch.

SP, Surrey

A. A book which guides us through the etiquette of shooting is Rosie Nickerson's *How to be Asked Again*. It is the duty of all guns to encourage and introduce newcomers to shooting and it is always disappointing to hear of resistance in this area.

Rosie Nickerson offers advice when sharing a peg with an inexperienced game-shot. Always ensure the shoot knows well in advance that you are bringing a guest rather than springing a surprise at the last moment. It should be made clear to the shoot captain that you will not both be shooting from the same peg at the same time. Shooting simultaneously is not only potentially dangerous but unfair to the other guns. Your suggestion of shooting the first three drives to familiarise the inexperienced gun in shooting etiquette and letting him shoot the next three seems spot on and a safer option.

Shooting Manners

Q. Is there a book published on shooting etiquette? I received a ribbing from fellow guns last year when I was rather competitive with my hostess, shooting birds that were probably mine but could have been hers. I don't wish to make more mistakes this year.

CVL, Honiton, Devon

A. *How to be Asked Again* by Rosie Nickerson (Quiller Publishing) is a good guide. Rosie says one unwritten rule is, 'Do not rain down birds on your host or hostess' or any neighbour for that matter. If your bird lands too close to someone apologise promptly and try not to do it again.

Try to earn a reputation as a shot who is generous and fun to shoot next to. It would be worthwhile to show a modicum of restraint. Let your neighbour, regardless of who she or he is – male or female, host or hostess – have a free rein occasionally to go for the birds that are between you, and don't raise your gun to every single bird. If your neighbour misses, don't feel you have to go for an eye-wipe as this is humiliating particularly for a gun who is perhaps not as accomplished as you. It is a good idea to call out 'Good shot!' now and again when you think it is deserved.

If your neighbour appears to be dithering you could occasionally shout 'Yours!' Everyone appreciates being left a few birds and no one likes a greedy, competitive shot.

From the Archives

The following appeared in *The Field* in January 1899.

COVERTS

Q. Would you kindly inform me what you consider the best covert to plant in woods for pheasant and wood-cock? My coverts are chiefly Scotch fir and spruce, and have little or no undergrowth in them. They stand nearly all on hills, or you may say, moorland, and the soil is peat or turf soil, and wet. Would you advise willows (withies), furze, sloe bushes, and bilberries? Briars do not seem to do very well with me.

LM

A. All you name are useful, and, like all native plants, may be depended on in hard weather. Always sow furze and broom out of hand – never plant – as they come well from seed sown direct where they are wanted. It is difficult to get covert under woods of dense evergreen trees. Grown together, as they ought to be, and are in German forests, it is sometimes dark under the trees at noon.

You should make breaks here and there in places where plants that require the sun can grow, varying the woodland a bit by adding waste corners and planting more attractive covert plants.

Shooting Stockings

Q. I am looking for a knitting pattern for shooting stockings. Please can you help?

JB, Horley, Surrey

A. I cannot find a pattern specifically for shooting stockings but I have found one for kilt socks, which I think would suffice. It gives designs for a stag's head, thistle and cable border with or without a garter rib in double knitting.

It is a Patons pattern (number 3285) and any wool shop that does not already stock it should be able to order it for you.

To Dress a Pigeon

Q. I believe it is possible to dress out a pigeon without the use of a knife. What is the technique?

AL-J, Anslow, Staffs

A. John Humphreys tells me that you need to use the Greenhill Method, invented by Cambridgeshire countryman Ron Greenhill. Using this you can prepare a woodpigeon, oven-ready, in 15 seconds without tools or knives.

Grasp the bird in your left hand and, with your right screw round and pull off the wing where it joins the body. Repeat the process for the second wing. Holding the bird breast uppermost in your left hand grasp the crop area between wishbone and head and rip off with a downward motion. A small triangular hole will appear at the top of the sternum. Insert both thumbs and break open the bird lengthways. The back of the bird, complete with innards, will still be attached to the breast skin which you peel off in one movement. You are left with the breast bone with the breast meat intact and a few loose feathers adhering, soon removed. Work over a dustbin with a liner inside. A beginner should be able to manage a bird well within a minute, while experts can do it in seconds.

Shooting Advice

Q. We have just helped three youngsters begin their shooting careers. As part of this we gave them each a copy of the celebrated *A Father's Advice To His Son*. Can you tell me who wrote it and when, and anything about the author?

JB-N, Kloof, South Africa

A. Mark Beaufoy wrote it for his son, Henry, when he was given his 28-bore as a Christmas present in 1902. Mark Beaufoy ran a vinegar and British winemaking company, Beaufoy & Co, based in Kennington. He was also was the Liberal MP for the Kennington Division of Lambeth from 1889 until defeated in 1895, and was an Alderman of the London County Council. He was born in 1854 and died in 1922.

A Fat Pheasant

Q. On 25 November a cock pheasant was shot here which weighed 2.3kg (5lb). Is this a record and, if not, what is?

FNHW, Morpeth

A. There does not seem to be a record laid down anywhere and it is difficult to say what is a standard weight for pheasants as so much depends on the quantity and quality of food available.

The normal weight of a cock pheasant varies from 1.3 to 1.5kg (3 to 3½lb) and a hen is usually 1.1kg (2½lb), but birds whose diets are supplemented with maize may easily weigh over 2.3kg (5lb).

A Popular Bore

Q. With the recent trend towards 1oz game loads, I would be intrigued to learn what the pros and cons are between the increasingly popular 20-bore and the 12-bore for game-shooting. I am interested in the differences in range, killing power and increased sportingness.

RWF, Sheffield

A. It is true that 20-bores are becoming more popular in game-shooting and clay-shooting. However, it should be stressed that to get the best value out of a 20-bore, the user must be a good shot.

As regards the load used, many believe that 1oz loads are a little too strong in a 20-bore side-by-side, causing unnecessary recoil and that you might just as well use a 12-bore. On the other hand, the Americans happily use 1½oz magnum loads in 20-bores for their game-shooting.

Sub-1oz loads – ⅞oz, for example – are quite adequate for the job, bearing in mind the user is a good shot. If you are going to use a 20-bore side-by-side, try a 30in, as opposed to the traditional 28in, gun. It has better pointing characteristics and will slow the swing down to a better pace.

For details of cartridges you should contact one of the major manufacturers who will be able to provide the full specifications.

Legal

Note

It should be noted that the law relating to field sports and the countryside is regularly updated and the following applies to the time of publication. Latest information can be checked with BASC, Marford Mill. Wrexham LL12 OHL.

Whose Shooting Rights?

Q. We are relative newcomers to the countryside and don't necessarily know all the rural ways. Our neighbour has a small piece of land. At the end of a day's shooting on a local shoot, he appears from his house and walks his dog round his field and shoots any pheasants that have escaped the main shoot – a single drive, as such. While we don't disapprove, we wonder whether it is legal.

PC, by e-mail

A. Occasionally houses that used to belong to a large estate, but were sold off with land, had their shooting rights withheld, but provided the neighbour has the right to shoot on his land then, yes, this is legal. The British Association of Shooting and Conservation explains that pheasants are wild birds and once released they no longer belong to anyone. Therefore, as long as it is not a Sunday or dark, your neighbour has the right to shoot the pheasants if they are on his land. If a shot bird falls on to your land, technically it is yours, and the neighbour has to have your permission to pick it from your premises, otherwise in the eyes of the law he is trespassing.

Killer Kites

Q. I bought 12 point of lay Black Rock chickens last September and I am now left with four because the red kites keep killing them. Am I entitled to shoot the kites for control purposes?

VA, Glos

A. The short answer is no. The red kite has been given the strongest degree of legal protection under Schedule 1 of the Wildlife and Countryside Act (1981) which states that it is an offence to take, injure or kill a red kite or to take, damage or destroy its nest, eggs or young. It is also an offence intentionally to disturb the birds close to their nest during the breeding season. Violation of the law can bring fines of up to £5,000 per offence and, in severe cases, a prison sentence of up to six months. Red kites are protected at all times as they were near extinction at the end of the 19th century. A few pairs survived in Wales and in 1989 a decision was made to bring them back to England and Scotland. They are breeding successfully at a few sites across the country, but are still under threat, hence the tight control. All birds released as part of the reintroduction scheme have been fitted with coloured wing tags and the RSPB is asking for sightings to be reported to the website www.euring.org to help monitor their movements and the spread of the kite population. To protect chickens from the kites one has to provide a covered run or keep them in a coop.

Permitted Possession

Q. Following on from the article *Your handsome blade and you* (December issue) would you be able to advise on what knives are legal to carry and under what circumstances in the UK. I would hate to fall foul of the law.

GM, Stogumber Somerset

A. In the UK it is against the law to carry a knife or offensive weapon in a public place unless you have a good reason. If you carry a knife to make yourself feel safer but don't intend to use it then you are also committing a crime. The Criminal Justice Act 1988 states that it is illegal to carry any sharp or bladed instrument in a public place with the exception of a folding penknife with a blade that is less than 7.62cm (3in) in length, which means no fixed blades. It is also illegal to carry a lock knife, due to its mechanism which locks the blade in position when fully extended. This knife is not an offensive weapon if used in the manner for which it was designed, but if found in your possession in a public place it would be an offence. It is up to the person in possession of such a knife to prove that he has a good reason for carrying it.

Who's Guilty?

Q. When recently staying with friends we found a dead dove in the garden. It seemed to have been plucked but its wings were still intact. This was obviously not the work of a cat and we wondered whether it was killed by a peregrine.

EB, by e-mail

A. This sounds like the work of a bird of prey, probably a sparrowhawk, as it would be very unusual for a peregrine to visit a domestic garden. Male and female sparrowhawks vary in size and quite often take different sized prey. The males take smaller birds up to the size of a blackbird while the females go for large birds including doves and woodpigeon.

The easiest way to identify whether the dove was taken by a bird of prey is to look at how the feathers have been plucked from the bird. Feathers plucked by a bird of prey will often have a split in their shaft where the raptor has, pulled them out. However, it is usually the larger feathers such as the wing feathers that show these features.

Bee Sensible

Q. If we place our beehives in woodland near a public footpath would we be liable if someone was stung?

SF, by e-mail

A. The British Beekeepers' Association (BBKA) says that responsible beekeepers would be foolish to place their hives in such a public place.

Bees need a clear flight path from their hives and would inevitably collide with and scare walkers. It advises anyone who keeps bees to have full insurance cover, the BBKA's own policy covers liability up to £5 million.

Register online at www.britishbee.org.uk for more advice on keeping bees. You can request a free apiary visit from you local inspector.

Chicken Killer

Q. My neighbour has a two-year-old springer spaniel that she has trained to use as a gundog. Last summer the dog attacked and killed two of our free-range hens. Recently it has started attacking again. This is a delicate situation. In each case the owner had taken the dog for a walk on the lane and in the fields. As a gundog it has many years of usefulness but its behaviour near to home needs sorting. What can be done to cure or retrain a chicken killer? Your advice, please.

KD, by e-mail

A. Your neighbour has broken various laws. Persistent stock killing is very serious and your neighbour is behaving in an anti-social way in allowing her dog to do this repeatedly. The dog needs to be kept on a lead near stock and if she refuses to do this then you should contact the dog warden attached to your local authority or police station. The dog warden will then visit the owner and explain the various options open to her, including where to find local dog-training classes. The Kennel Club should also be able to recommend a local gundog training club.

The dog doesn't have a useful life ahead as a gundog if it behaves like this – it wouldn't be welcome on any respectable shoot. The main law that may be relevant in this instance is the Dogs (Protection of Livestock) Act 1953, which gives livestock owners the right to shoot dogs that are harassing their animals if on agricultural land. This applies to any domestic livestock – goats, pigs, horses, sheep, poultry and cattle.

Cattle and Dogs

Q. I walk my well-behaved mongrel on the lead through a field in which there is a registered footpath in regular use. The field is now pasture for Charolais cattle, and on a recent walk the cattle charged me. I had to release my dog from the lead and jump the fence to escape.

Though I explained what happened, the cattle's owner has threatened to shoot my dog the next time it is off the lead on his property. Is there a law to protect the walker in instances like this?

SB, Ludlow Shropshire

A. There does not appear to be one law that covers this situation. The majority of incidents when cattle charge seem to occur when they are protecting their young. The Local Government Association, Ramblers, the National Farmers' Union, the Country Land & Business Association, the Health and Safety Executive and The Royal Society for the Protection of Accidents at a meeting agreed that releasing your dog is the correct way to behave in these circumstances, though they are unable to legislate against livestock owners who take it upon themselves to shoot the dog.

The Countryside Alliance (CA) says there are three major things in your defence: it is illegal to shoot a dog if it is not pestering livestock; you have a lawful right to pass uninterrupted on a public footpath; and under the Animals Act of 1971 if livestock owners know the animals to be dangerous then the onus is on them to show they have acted responsibly by protecting walkers, otherwise they can be prosecuted. If you are a member of the CA it can offer a certain amount of free legal advice.

All these major countryside agents recommend contacting the police where threats are involved to ensure a peaceful and satisfactory outcome.

Field Footpaths

Q. Is there is a time limit for a farmer to leave his field ploughed before reinstating a smooth footpath across it? I am fairly elderly and find the deep plough impossible to walk on. One neighbouring farmer makes sure the footpath across his field is walkable within days while another leaves it for as long as possible. Can you help and suggest the best way of handling this?

CJ, Suffolk

A. The Rights of Way Act 1990 places a number of duties on farmers in respect of footpaths crossing agricultural land. If the cultivation of a cross-field path cannot conveniently be avoided, the farmer has 14 days from the first disturbance to restore the surface of the path and to make its line apparent on the ground. In any subsequent operations this is reduced to 24 hours.

Glyn French, the area rights of way manager for Suffolk County Council, explained that some farmers are better than others at accepting and complying with their legal obligations. A walker can approach the farmer direct or alternatively contact the county council rights of way office. The county council has powers of enforcement but most farmers will reinstate paths once they have been reminded. For further advice contact Suffolk County Council on 0845 606 6067.

Whose Right?

Q. At a shoot in Hampshire recently we had a footpath 27 metres (30yds) behind us. During a drive I noticed a man on a motorcycle observing us. I was surprised to see him get off his bike and load some fallen pheasants into his jacket, and as I approached he quickly departed. As the birds were on the public footpath was he entitled to pick them up, or did I have the right to stop him and ask him to return the birds? To whom does fallen game belong if it lands on a public right of way?

MB, Hawkedon, Suffolk

A. Before anything else is considered, it must be noted that by riding a motorcycle on a public footpath the person in question was breaking the law.

Tom Blades, BASC's Head of Gamekeeping, offers the following advice. Once game has been released into the wild there is no restriction on where it may roam. The principle of this, whereby wild animals and birds are free to go from one person's land to another, remaining ownerless (therefore exempt from being 'stolen'), has long been accepted.

If game is shot and lands dead on a highway, the owner of that highway would have first claim to it. Where game is shot and lands on a public right of way that is adjacent to or crosses the land upon which the gun has authority to be, the gun would have the right to it. If a gun wounds the game which then runs or falls alive on to neighbouring property and he does not have authority to enter, he could potentially commit a poaching offence. If a bird lands dead on the neighbouring property and he enters to retrieve it without permission, a civil offence of trespass could be committed. If the gun were to enter with a firearm then a criminal offence would be committed.

Love Thy Neighbour

Q. Could you please enlighten me as regards the law if a dangerous tree on our neighbour's land falls and damages our house.

CL, Gloucestershire

A. If a tree growing on your neighbour's land should fall and damage your house in a storm, wind or bad weather it would be regarded in law as 'an act of God' for which your neighbour cannot be held responsible. Apparently you have no redress. If you feel that the tree or its parts are a danger to your house or property it would be useful to either talk or write to your neighbour to point this out and explain your fears.

You can legally cut back branches or roots at any point where they cross the boundary line and so trespass into your garden. To cut back growth farther into his living space you would need his permission. Any matter removed is his property and should be returned to him.

Index